This book is to be returned on or before
the last date stamped below.

The Scottish Students' Song : Book

PVBLISHED FOR
THE.:: SCOTTISH
STUDENTS.SONG
BOOK.COMMITTEE.L^{TD}

BY
BAYLEY & FERGVSON
LONDON: 2:GREAT
MARLBOROUGH:ST,
GLASGOW:54:QVEEN
STREET.:

Introduction.

THE man that hath no music in his soul, as our great dramatist says, is fit for murders and con-
spiracies and for every evil work of blackest dye. Many notable things the spirit who
is the impersonation of evil can do ; generally, indeed, he must be a clever fellow to
plant himself with any success against the array of good in the world that is against him ;
he must be cunning, he may be witty, he will be strong in sneers and sarcasm, and even
mount to the sublime of defiant eloquence, as we find him in Milton. But he cannot sing.
And this indeed is only quite natural ; for, if the music which has its seat in the ear, consists
essentially in the agreement of sweet sounds and in the abolition of all discords, the music of
the soul which is its correlative in the moral world, must be essentially the harmony of all
pure, noble, and joyous emotions, to the exclusion of all such moral discords as are expressed
by the words, faction, jealousy, wrath, malice, and all uncharitableness ; and so, as a matter
of history, we find that not only songs properly so called, but all forms of intellectual and
moral life, were sung and not written ; in fact, were composed in an age when for all the
higher purposes of intelligent expression prose was unknown. The physical philosophy of
Empedocles, no less than the golden verses of Pythagoras, were sung, not said ; and the
doctrine of metres, according to which Latin and Greek poetry is scanned, was part of the
science of music, not of spoken notation. And even to the latest days, when writing became
common, and prose the general medium of intellectual currency, we find that the word Μουσική,
which with us is confined to the harmony of sweet sounds as the luxury of the ear, was the
general Greek term of what we call literature, including music as a special department sub-
ordinate to the dominant element of inspired intelligence.

In modern times, notwithstanding the immense multiplication of prose books, and the
general habit of reading, the divine art of music has not failed to assert triumphantly its
natural sovereignty in all regions where life is most enjoyable and man most noble. In the
earliest and best ages of Hebrew history, as in the case of Miriam, David, and Elisha, and
the schools of the prophets, the close alliance that existed between music and an essentially
ethical religion stands prominently out : and the Christian Church, through its long story of
nearly two thousand years, however opposed to Judaism in other respects, has been, with very
few exceptions, faithful to this holy alliance between a saintly life and sweet sounds. And we
may safely say, without any disparagement to Chalmers and other great masters of pulpit
eloquence, that no sermons ever preached so powerfully bring forth the fulness of devout
emotion in the soul as the oratorios, anthems, and hymns of our great musical composers.

Next to reverence for the great Source of our being, love of country, or as the Germans
more significantly call it, the Fatherland, presents itself as the natural steam power to set the
machinery of elevated musical expression in motion : and in this department, though no doubt
the Greeks, in the grand structure of their sacred operas, called tragedies, excel all moderns,
we have yet in our popular songs of patriotic and warlike achievement no small compensation
for the lack of that grand union of poetry, piety, patriotism, and song. On the banks of the
Elbe and the Rhine our Teutonic cousins, the Germans, have consecrated and embalmed for
all time the glorious achievements of the Liberation War of 1813, in the form of a contemporary series of popular songs * ; in England the hero of the Nile and Trafalgar is the
central figure of a series of nautical songs unequalled in the history of literature ; while in
Scotland the musical memory of Bannockburn and Stirling Brig will, it is hoped, long continue
to nourish in the breasts of Scotsmen that self-respect and manly independence, without which
no people can look for honourable recognition from abroad.

But it is not only in moments of great national uprising and historic achievement marked by
such names as Marathon, Bannockburn, and Trafalgar, that the Lyrical Muse finds a field for
her ennobling inspirations ; from the familiar drama of daily life she is cunning to pick up

---

* War Songs of the Germans, by J. S. B.—Edinburgh, 1870.

themes, which, when transmuted by her magic, if less brilliant, are sometimes more pleasing, more profitable, and more permanent than far more lofty odes. In this department, while all honour is due to the Germans, as the most musical of modern nations,* perhaps the seat of honour must be given to the Scotch, in whose popular songs dramatic point, picturesque scenery, passion, pathos, simplicity, nature, grace, humour, and practical wisdom unite with the most delicate music, and the most musical of all popular dialects, to form an artistic compound as perfect in its sphere as the Odes of Pindar or the Choral Songs of the Greek drama.

To the scenes of daily life that are naturally most fitted for lyrical treatment, the life of the young men at our Universities should no doubt contribute its significant share. But in Students' Songs, strictly so called, and student life musically treated, our lyrical repertory hitherto shews a face only a little better than an absolute blank. It is otherwise in Germany. In that country songs of a specifically academic type occupy a distinct and generally recognised place in the lyrical literature of the country.† What the reasons may be for this deficiency of music in our academical presentation, one may partly guess. Perhaps John Bull, with all his good qualities, is not such a musical animal as the German, delighting more in strong blows than in nice sentiment; and his brother Sandy, made naturally of no less excellent stuff, and from whom, considering his antecedents, better things might have been expected, has undoubtedly suffered in the artistic side of his nature by the unfortunate divorce between religion and the fine arts, which grew up in him as a reaction against the despotic ceremonialism of the Stuarts. But these days are past. Notwithstanding the sour religiosity and dogmatic rigidity of certain Presbyterian Doctors in the far North, anthems and hymns and organs present themselves now without offence even in the most distinctly free of Free Church places of worship; and any taint of unmusical severity which our academical youth might have inherited from the stern Calvinism of those times may now be considered as passed away, and the present volume of popular and patriotic School and University Songs, issued by the representatives of the students of Scotland, will help to inaugurate a new era in our academical life, when piety shall no longer be associated with gloomy looks, nor music with frivolity.

JOHN STUART BLACKIE.

May, 1891.

---

* (1) Germania: Volksgesangbuch von Ludwig Erk. Berlin: Otto Jarte.
  (2) Orpheus ad Romos, von Pr. E——r. Meissen: Gœdsche.

† (1) Allgemeines Deutsches Commersbuch, by Silcher and Erk. 15 Auflage
  (2) Studenten-Lieder, mit Bildern und Singweisen: by Richter and Massilner.

To match with this I have in my library only a small volume of Harrow Songs.

J. S. B.

Editors' Preface.

IT is ten years now, or so, since the smallest of the Universities of Scotland set itself bravely to the task of preparing, not for itself only, but for the other Universities as well, a collection of Students' Songs. It is surprising that the task was not faced before. Other countries, some of them not more musical than ours, had shown the example of what might be done. We do not know whether any other Continental countries possess Song Books such as the well-known *Commersbuch* of the Germans. But America has many. Canada has two at least; and in the United States, where Universities are legion, collections of Students' Songs are very numerous. That Scotland should have been so long content with none is strange. But the need for one was strongly felt, and to St. Andrews belongs the honour of the first attempt to meet it. It was fitting that in such an undertaking St. Andrews should lead the way, for in the happy and genial social atmosphere which is, so to say, one of the qualities of its defects, one of the compensations for its smallness, song has always flourished there. "The taint of unmusical severity," which Professor Blackie lamented in "our academical youth," has never been, within living memory at least, a characteristic of St. Andrews. Enthusiasm for song has long been so; and it was that enthusiasm that led St. Andrews, first among the Universities, to conceive and to undertake the preparation of such a book as this.

In that hardy enterprise one of the Editors of this book was mainly concerned, and he remembers how hopeful at first it seemed. But the impecuniosity which has dogged the little University for centuries and wrecked so many of its brave schemes, brought this one also to shipwreck. For after all, there are some things in which it does need more than the will to find the way, in this world where it is only money that "answereth all things."

But the hope that had carried the scheme so far was not to be defeated by a mere sordid question of pounds, shillings, and pence. An appeal was made to the other Universities; they agreed to co-operate in the enterprise; the present Editors were appointed to carry it out; and success was in sight at last. Difficulties, however, were not removed, nor indeed much lessened. The Editors found that they were expected to make bricks without straw. It was hard enough to produce a book with scanty materials to work upon, and discouraging enough to do it in face of general prophecies of failure: it was still more hard to discover that they were expected to do it without means. But when difficulties were being grappled with at any rate, one more or less mattered little. Enough money was found by the Editors themselves to do what was necessary. If they could not afford to pay a competent musician to arrange or revise the settings of the songs, why, they could make shift to do the work after a fashion themselves. And it was done, after endless trouble and worry; but done at last. The book bristled with imperfections. The critics could have made very merry at its expense had they cared. But most of them were charitable enough to welcome it, if not for its own excellences, at least as a step towards something better. And in that view of it the Editors found consolation too.

The book leapt at once into a great popularity, in spite of all its defects. As soon as possible, when money enough for the purpose was in hand, it was revised and enlarged. Then its circulation became wider still. Everyone who saw the book wished to possess a copy; and without advertisement, simply by those who knew the book recommending it to others, and by its own recommendation to those who saw others use it, it has made its way amazingly far afield, till now there are few "places where they sing" in Scotland where it is not in familiar use, and throughout England, and in India, and in many British colonies and settlements, wherever, indeed, our countrymen are found, it is becoming widely known, and, beyond all question, prized. That the book has been accorded a welcome so far surpassing their most sanguine expectations, has been most gratifying to the Editors, and has been to them ample compensation for the great expense of trouble and of time, which it has cost them. They trust that this new edition, revised, greatly enlarged and improved, will commend the book to a still wider favour.

The songs of which the book is made up are of the most miscellaneous character; and the Editors hope that it is unnecessary to explain why this is so. The tastes of students are endlessly various; and the tastes of all had to be kept in view. Had the Editors been entirely free, and guided by their own tastes only, the collection would have been a little different at least: there are songs included which some of them would fain have parted with or never have admitted at all, but which are so firmly established in the favour of a large number of students that they could not be left out. If the Editors could not follow their own judgment with unrestricted freedom, still less could they follow freely the opinions of their critics. Indeed, they would have been in a strange quandary had they even attempted to do so; for the counsels that were offered them and pressed upon them as certain to redeem the book from all its shortcomings were amusing in their utter and hopeless diversity. Songs, for example, which some condemned most roundly, were in many instances precisely those which a majority most emphatically demanded to have retained. The Editors, considering that in their work they were acting as trustees for the students, aimed at making the book acceptable and useful, not to one class only, but in a measure to all. Thus, those whose tastes are most severe and those whose likings are most diametrically the opposite will alike find in the collection many songs to please them; and if the whole book is not what they would have it, perhaps they will complain less if they remember that the contents are so diverse because "such and so various are the tastes of men."

The co-operation of the Students' Representative Councils was invited by the Editors at the beginning of their work upon this edition, in the hope that students' opinion as to the existing book might thus be fully elicited, and that not suggestions as to possible improvements only, but contributions also, might in this way be plentifully secured. The result was very disappointing. Perhaps it was their superabundance of confidence in the Editors that made two of the Councils take practically no steps in the matter: it is certain at least that one of them suggested one solitary song, and did nothing else whatever, and that the other did not so much as suggest even one. More was done by the two remaining Councils, and the suggestions that came from Edinburgh were especially serviceable, though most of the songs proposed for inclusion were valuable copyrights, which could not on any terms be obtained. Beyond that, practically no help was offered by students, either past or present. Vague and general criticisms were abundant enough, but actual definite help was not. The new contributions which have been secured were not offered, but had to be sought. If, therefore, the songs of a specifically academic type still bear a regrettably small proportion to the miscellaneous contents of the book, the Editors can only express regret that to their appeal for contributions of this kind so slight a response was given, and their hope that before another edition is prepared, that appeal, which they now renew, will bring such materials in abundance to their hands.

For this edition the music of the book has throughout been very thoroughly revised. Much of the work was done by Mr. W. AUGUSTUS BARRATT; and still more by Mr. J. KENYON LEES; to both of whom, as well as to the others who have given help in this part of the work, the Editors are much indebted for the care and sympathy and understanding with which their work was done. It is hoped that now all the songs will be found to be well within the range of average voices, and the accompaniments sufficiently full and effective, without being unduly difficult for even unskilful amateurs to play.

The Editors have again to express their indebtedness to the contributors of whose help acknowledgment was made in former editions (see Prefaces in Appendix), and now also to many others whose co-operation has been secured in this edition for the first time: to Mr. RUDYARD KIPLING, Mr. QUILLER COUCH, Mr. CHARLES BAXTER (for the executors of the late ROBERT LOUIS STEVENSON), Sir WILLIAM GEDDES, etc.

Efforts were made to enrich the book by the inclusion of various copyright songs. But many publishers proved obdurate, and would neither for love nor money grant the necessary permission. To the following firms the obligation is therefore the greater for their courtesy in making arrangements by which the Editors have been enabled to include certain copyright songs, of which special acknowledgment is made in the places where they appear: Messrs. NOVELLO, EWER & Co.; Messrs. CHAPPELL & Co.; Messrs. A. & S. NORDHEIMER, Toronto, Canada; Messrs. G. RICORDI & Co., Milan; Messrs. E. ASCHERBERG & Co.; Mr. WALTER WHITTINGHAM; Messrs. FRANCIS, DAY, & HUNTER; Messrs. WILLIAM BLACKWOOD & SON; EDWIN ASHDOWN, Ltd.; Messrs. R. COCKS & Co.; Mr. ARCHIBALD SINCLAIR, etc.

No effort has been spared by Editors and publishers alike to guard against any infringement of copyright. If, in spite of their vigilance, they have transgressed, they trust that an error made so unwittingly will be willingly forgiven.

November, 1897.

MILLAR PATRICK, M.A., St. Andrews.
WILLIAM NELSON, Glasgow.
J. MALCOLM BULLOCH, M.A., Aberdeen.
A. STODART WALKER, M.B., F.R.C.P., Edinburgh.

Preface.

SINCE the first issue of this edition the original Editors have resigned office. The present Editors in taking up the work cannot refrain from alluding to the conspicuous services which their predecessors have rendered to Student Song. These services have already been recognised by the Students of the four Scottish Universities at the Inter-Universities Conference of 1900. But we feel that we must take this fresh opportunity of placing on record the gratitude which all Students owe to the Rev. MILLAR PATRICK and his colleagues, for their untiring labours in the interest of this Book.

It has been found necessary to carry on the work of the Book in the future by means of a Company. In this Company there are Eight Shareholders in all, each of whom either has been or is a member of one of the Scottish Universities, two being of St. Andrews, two of Glasgow, two of Aberdeen, and two of Edinburgh, and arrangements have been made whereby this will always be the case.

The new position of matters therefore is that instead of the Students of the four Universities being represented by delegates from their respective Councils to the annual Inter-Universities Conference of which the Editors jointly were a Committee, they are now represented by the Shareholders of the Company. By this means a perpetual trusteeship is, in effect, created for behoof of the whole body of Students of the Scottish Universities.

The present Editors enter on their duties in the hope that they will be able to maintain the best traditions of that Student effort which is ever given so cheerfully and spontaneously to any University project.

Wo man singt, da lass Dich ruhig nieder:
Böse Menschen haben keine Lieder.

—*German Proverb*

Index of Sections.

SONGS OF THE GOWN.

"*I have a little studied physic; but now, I'm all for music....as Plato holds your music and so does wise Pythagoras, I take it is your true rapture.*"

BEN JONSON, *Volpone, iii, 2.*

GAUDEAMUS.

Student-Song
of the Middle Ages.

Arr. by Sir Herbert S. Oakeley, Mus. Doc., (1876.)

INTEGER VITÆ.

Q. Horatii Flacci Lib. I. Carm. XXII.

J. J. Flemming.

3.

Namque me silva lupus in Sabina,
Dum meam canto Lalagen, et ultra
Terminum curis vagor expeditis,
Fugit inermem.

4.

Quale portentum neque militaris
Daunias latis alit æsculetis;
Nec Jubæ tellus generat leonum
Arida nutrix.

5.

Pone me, pigris ubi nulla campis
Arbor æstiva recreatur aura;
Quod latus mundi nebulæ malusque
Jupiter urget.

6.

Pone sub curru nimium propinqui
Solis, in terra domibus negata;
Dulce ridentem Lalagen amabo,
Dulce loquentem.

ALMA MATER.

Words by Prof. Sir Douglas Maclagan, M.D., etc.   Music by Em. Prof. Sir Herbert Oakeley, Mus. Doc., etc.

(Second setting, 1884.)

D.C. for V. 2.

** The orchestral score is in the key of A flat. Two bars side drums, (Solo), and half bar precede the entry of the voices.

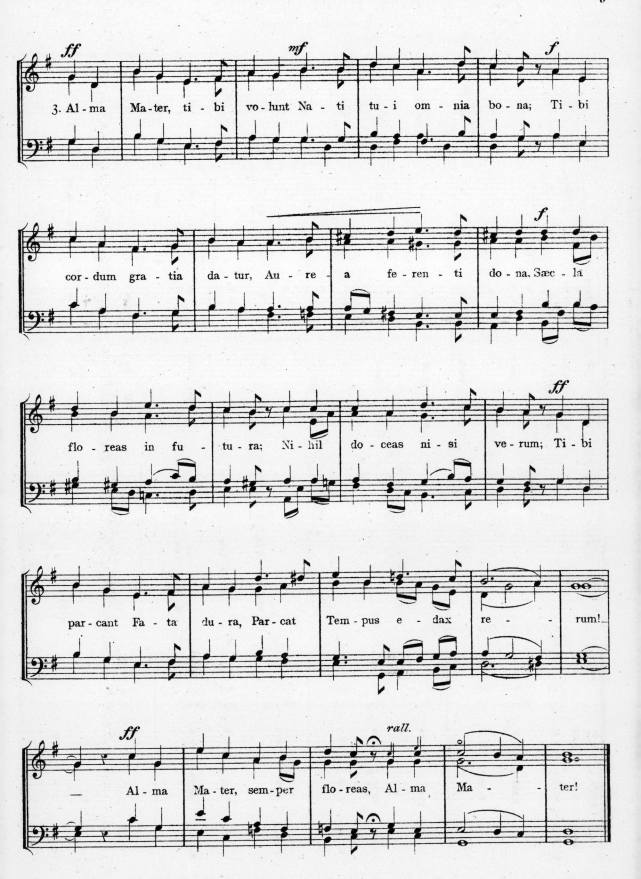

FROM HIGH OLYMPUS.

Vom hoh'n Olymp.

German Words,(1795.)
Translation by Prof. John Stuart Blackie,(1841.)

Air by Heinrich Christian Schnoor (1801.)
Arr: by W. Augustus Barratt. (1897.)

Maestoso.

1. Vom hoh'n O - lymp he - rab ward uns die Freu - de, Ward uns der
1. From high O - lym - pus, Jove's free boun - ty gave us Life's fleet - ing

Ju - gendtraum be - scheert; Drum,trau - te Brü - der,trotzt dem blas - sen
good, youth's fleet - er joy; There - fore, dear bro - thers, let no fear en -

Nei - de, Der uns - re Ju - gend Freu - den stört.
slave us, Scorn change - ful chance, hard fate de - fy.

CHORUS. last verse pp.

Fei - er - lich schal - le der Ju - bel - ge - sang
So - lemn - ly bil - low the strong stu - dent - glee;

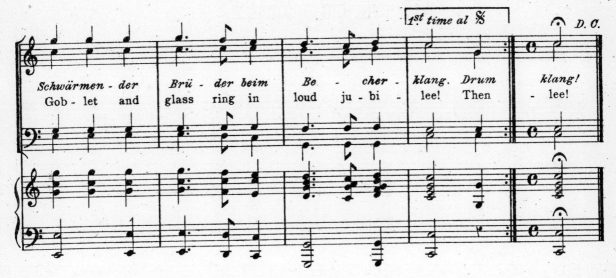

Schwärmen - der Brü - der beim Be - cher - klang. Drum klang!
Gob - let and glass ring in loud ju - bi - lee! Then - lee!

1st time al ℈. D. C.

2.

Versenkt in's Meer der jugendlichen Wonne,
Lacht uns der Freuden hohe Zahl,
Bis einst am späten Abend uns die Sonne
Nicht mehr entzückt mit ihrem Strahl.
Feierlich etc.

2.

When life is young, unnumber'd joys before us
Flash, and around mirth's wild waves roar;
But when cold eve her thin grey veil draws o'er us,
We greet thy light, blithe sun, no more.
Solemnly etc.

3.

So lang' es Gott gefällt, ihr lieben Brüder,
Woll'n wir uns dieses Lebens freu'n,
Und fällt der Vorhang einst auch uns hernieder,
Vergnügt uns zu den Vätern reih'n.
Feierlich etc.

3.

While God's high will extends life's rapid measure,
Drink joy's full cup, fan flaming fires;
But when the curtain falls, depart with pleasure,
March with the word, sleep with your sires.
Solemnly etc.

4.

Herr Brüder, trink' auf's Wohlsein deiner Schönen,
Die deiner Jugend Traum belebt,
Lass', ihr zu Ehr', ein flottes Hoch ertönen,
Dass ihr's durch jede Nerve bebt!
Feierlich etc.

4.

Brother, this cup to her thy heart doth name her;-
Fill to the maid that loves thee, fill!
Let loud Vivats with echoes blithe acclaim her,
Till in each nerve her bosom thrill.
Solemnly etc.

5.

Ist einer unsrer Brüder dann geschieden,
Vom blassen Tod gefordert ab,
So weinen wir und wünschen Ruh' und Frieden
In unsers Bruders stilles Grab.
Wir weinen und wünschen Ruhe hinab
In unsers Bruders stilles Grab.

5.

And when pale death a brother's bond shall sever,
And Nature claim what Nature gave,
We weep and pray, may peace and rest be ever
On our dear brother's silent grave.
We weep, and we pray o'er our brother's cool grave,
May God keep thy soul in His peace, brother brave!

THE CROCODILE.

Paraphrased, on the occasion of Professor Blackie's visit to Egypt in 1879, from E. Geibel's well-known German song "Ein lust'ger Musikante spazierte einst am Nil," by Professor Julius Eggeling, Ph. D.

THE CROCODILE.

I.

A famous Scotch Professor was walking by the Nile,
O tempora! O mores!
When from the muddy water crept a beastly crocodile,
O tempora! O mores!
It gaped for to devour him, plaid, philabeg an' a'.
O tempo-tempora! Juch-heirassasasa!
We praise thee now and evermore, Dame Musica!

2.

He shriek'd ' ὤ μοι ψῦ ψῦ ποποι!' then forth a bagpipe drew,
O tempora! O mores!
And on that noble instrument sweet Gaelic tunes he blew,
O tempora! O mores!
Allegro, dolce, presto, – oh, how he did them blaw!
O tempo-tempora! Juch-heirassasasa!
We praise thee now and evermore, Dame Musica!

3.

And at the first melodious howl that from the bag did go,
O tempora! O mores!
The ugly brute began to trip the light fantastic toe,
O tempora! O mores!
Jig, reel, and waltz, and polka, and Highland fling an' a'!
O tempo-tempora! Juch-heirassasasa!
We praise thee now and evermore, Dame Musica!

4.

It gnashed its teeth, and hopped and skipped the sandy plain aroun',
O tempora! O mores!
Till with its waggling tail it knocked a lot o' pyramids doun,
O tempora! O mores!
For they have long been rickety, with mummies, bones, an' a'!
O tempo-tempora! Juch-heirassasasa!
We praise thee now and evermore, Dame Musica!

5.

And when he saw the pyramids had squashed the crocodill,
O tempora! O mores!
He turned into the nearest pub., his inner man to fill,
O tempora! O mores!
He sipped and quaffed Nile-water, an' whiskey, beer, an' a'!
O tempo-tempora! Juch-heirassasasa!
We praise thee now and evermore, Dame Musica!

6.

All genuine Scotch Professors like fish their liquor swill:
O tempora! O mores!
If this one has not ceased to drink, maybe he's drinking still;
O tempora! O mores!
And all good men drink with him, Greek, Teuton, Celt, an' a'!
O tempo-tempora! Juch-heirassasasa!
We praise thee now and evermore, Dame Musica!

DULCE DOMUM.

Moderato con moto.

Ascribed to John Reading. 17th Century.

1. Con - ci - na - mus, o So - da - les! E - ja! quid si - le - mus?
2. Ap - pro-pin-quat, ec - ce! fe - lix Ho - ra gau-di - o - rum:

No - bi - le can-ti - cum, Dul-ce me-los, Do - mum, Dul - ce Do - mum, re - so - ne - mus.
Post gra-ve tæ-di - um Ad-ve-nit om-ni - um Me - ta pe - ti - ta la - bo - rum.

CHORUS.

Do - mum, Do - mum, Dul - ce Do - mum, Do - mum, Do - mum, Dul - ce Do - mum,

Dul - ce, Dul - ce, Dul - ce Do - mum, Dul - ce Do - mum re - so - ne - mus.

3.
Musa! libros mitte, fessa;
Mitte pensa dura;
Mitte negotium;
Jam datur otium:
Me mea mittito cura.
    Domum, Domum, etc.

4.
Ridet annus, prata rident:
Nosque rideamus.
Jam repetit Domum
Daulias advena:
Nosque Domum repetamus.
    Domum, Domum, etc.

5.
Heu! Rogere! fer caballos:
Eja! nunc eamus;
Limen amabile,
Matris et oscula,
Suaviter et repetamus.
    Domum, Domum, etc.

6.
Concinamus ad Penates;
Vox et audiatur:
Phosphore! quid jubar,
Segnius emicans,
Gaudia nostra moratur?
    Domum, Domum, etc.

SHON CAMPBELL.

Words by W. A. Mackenzie.

Music by W. Augustus Barratt.

Rather slowly.

1. Shon Campbell went to Col-lege, Be-cause he want-ed to; He left the croft in Gair-loch To dive in Bain and Drew. Shon Camp-bell died at Col - lege When the sky of spring was blue.

2. Shon Campbell went to Col-lege, The pul-pit was his aim; By day and night he ground, For he was Hie - lan, dour, and game; The ses - sion was a hard one, Shon flick-er'd like a flame.

3. Shon Campbell went to Col - lege, And gave the ghost up there, At - tempt - ing six men's cram - ming On a mean and scan - ty fare; Three days the Ter - tians mourn'd for him, 'Twas all that they could spare.

Shon Camp-bell lies in

This song is published separately by Messrs. J. B. Cramer & Co., London.

Gair - loch, Un - hood-ed and un - gown'd, The green quad-ran-gle of the hills to watch his sleep pro - found, And the Gau-de-a - mus of the burns mak - ing a homely sound.

dim.

But when the Last Great Roll is call'd, And

cres.

f

13

"A MILE AN' A BITTOCK."

*Words by Robert Louis Stevenson.

Music by W. Augustus Barratt.

Andante moderato.

1. A mile an' a bit-tock, a mile or twa, A - bune the burn a - yont the law, Dav - ie an' Don-al' an Cher - lie an' a', Don - al' an' Cher - lie an'

2. Ane went hame wi' the i - ther, an' then The i - ther went hame wi' the i - ther twa men, An' baith wad re - turn him the ser - vice a - gain, wad re - turn him the ser - vice a -

CHORUS. *May be sung unaccompanied if desired.* D.C. for 2nd verse.

An' the müne was shin - in' clear - ly!

a',
gain,

*Words included by kind permission of Charles Baxter, Esq., for the late Mr Stevenson's Executors.

af - fa the sea, It blew the stars as clear's could be, It
sleep in his head, "The best o' frien's maun twine," he said; "I'm

blew in the een o' a' o' the three, It blew in the een o' a' o' the
wear - iet, an' here I'm a - wa' to my bed, An' here I'm a - wa' to my

An' the müne was shin-in' clear - ly!

three,
bed"

6. Twa o' then walk-in' an'
7. O years a - yont, O

LAURIGER HORATIUS.

A song of the Wandering Students of the Middle Ages.
Translation by John Addington Symonds.

I. Lau - ri - ger Ho - ra - ti - us, Quam dix - is - ti ve - rum:
I. *Lau-rel-crown'd Ho - ra - ti - us, True, how true, thy say - ing!*

"Fu - git, Eu - ro ci - ti - us, Tem - pus e - dax re - rum."
"Swift as wind flies o - ver us Time, de - vour - ing, slay - ing!"

U - bi - sunt, O! po - cu - la, Dul - ci - o - ra mel - le,
Where are oh! those gob - lets full Of wine, ho - ney - la - den,

Rix - æ, pax, et os - cu - la Ru - ben - tis pu - el - læ?
Smiles and tears, and bount - i - ful Lips of rud - dy maid - en?

2.

Crescit uva molliter
  Et puella crescit,
Sed poeta turpiter
  Sitiens canescit.
Quid juvat æternitas
  Nominis, amare
Nisi terræ filias
  Licet, et potare?

2.

Grows the young grape tenderly,
  And the maid is growing;
But the thirsty poet, see!
  Years on him are snowing!
What's the use on hoary curls,
  Of the bays undying?
If we may not kiss the girls,
  Drink while time's a-flying.

A MEDICAL MEDLEY.

Words by Dr. Richard J. A. Berry.

Music by G. T. Lowe.

Allegretto.

Largo.

1. Oh! listen while we ask in com-mon phra-se-ol-o-gy,

If you can tell me what's the mat-ter with the la-dy's car-di-ol-o-gy.

With feeling.

She seems in pain, so I sur-mise She's got an-gi-na

pect-or-is, Which fact (of course we don't tell lies) Taught much by Profs at

lec-ture is: As-so-ci-a-ted then with this, She may have o-ther

les-ions oh! End-ar-ter-it-is with sep-sis And some bac-ter-ial termo.

REFRAIN.

Oh! in sci-en-tif-ic terms and el-e-gant phil-ol-o-gy I've

tried my best to di-ag-nose the la-dy's car-di-ol-o-gy.

Largo. *pp*

Oh! Listen while I ask in com-mon phra-se-ol-o-gy

D. S.

If you can tell me what's the mat-ter with the la-dy's car-di-ol-o-gy.

D. S.

2.

Now as I know by rote all British Pharmacology,
I'll try again to diagnose my lady's cardiology:
    Perchance she has a murmur, oh!
    Or bruits of debility;
    With, possibly, a valve stenosed,
    From hidden causes rickety:
    The lesion may be functional,
    With "diabolics" in the neck;
    Organic or Congenital,
    A total Cyanotic wreck.
I feel that surely now this medical pathology
Has diagnosed, correctly too, my lady's cardiology.
Now as I know by rote all British Pharmacology
I'll try again to diagnose my lady's cardiology.

3.

I'm driven now to study cerebral neurology
For diagnostic symptoms of my lady's cardiology:
    In infancy perchance she had
    Severe rheumatic fever, oh!
    With meningitis very bad
    From want of salicylates, oh!
    Embolic processes set up
    Thrombosis and paralysis:
    A bad result! She had no cup-
    ping or Haemic analysis.
If still correct is not this song of anthropology
I must decline to diagnose my lady's cardiology.
I'm driven now to study cerebral neurology
For diagnostic symptoms of my lady's cardiology.

THE DOCTOR.

Words by Thomas Hood. (1798-1845.)

Music by Ernest Newton.

With spirit.

1. There once was a Doc-tor (No foe to the Proc-tor), A phy-sic con-coc-tor, Whose dose was so pat, How-ev-er it act-ed, One speech it ex-tract-ed, "Yes, yes," said the Doc-tor, "I meant it for that!" He meant it for that, He meant it for that; There's no doubt a-bout it, he

2

And first, all "unaisy,"
Like woman that's crazy,
In flies Mrs Casey_
   "Do come to poor Pat!
The blood's running faster!
He's torn off the plaster"_
"Yes, yes," said the doctor,
   "I meant it for that!"

3

Anon, with an antic
Quite strange and romantic,
A woman comes frantic_
   "What could you be at?
My darling dear Alick
You've sent him oxalic!"
"Yes, yes," said the doctor,
   "I meant it for that!"

4

Then in comes another,
Despatched by his mother,
A blubbering brother
   Who gives a rat-tat_
"Oh, poor little sister
Has licked off a blister!"
"Yes, yes," said the doctor,
   "I meant it for that!"

5

Now home comes the flunkey,
His own powder monkey,
But dull as a donkey_
   With basket and that_
"The draught for the squire, sir,
He chucked in the fire, sir."
"Yes, yes," said the doctor,
   "I meant it for that!"

6

The next is the pompous
Head-beadle, old Bumpus,
"Lord! here is a rumpus;
   That pauper, old Nat,
In some drunken notion
Has drunk up his lotion."
"Yes, yes," said the doctor,
   "I meant it for that!"

7

At last comes a servant,
In grief very fervent,
"Alas! Doctor Derwent,
   Poor master is flat!
He's drawn his last breath, sir,
That dose was his death, sir."
"Yes, yes," said the doctor,
   "I meant it for that!"

THE POCKET GRAY.

Words by John Malcolm Bulloch.

Music by Ernest Newton.

1. What Bohn is to the ne-o-phyte in arts, What keys are to the ma-the-ma-tic dolt, What spurs are to the trai-ner when he starts The break-ing of a dil-a-to-ry colt, This book is to the me-di-cal who smarts When grap-pling with an-a-to-my's ar-ray: Need I

tell you that the ti -tle of this *va de me cum* vi -tal Is the famous and fa mi liar Pock et

Gray? Need I tell you that the ti -tle of this *va de me cum* vi -tal Is the

fam ous and fa mi liar Pock et Gray? Gray.

2.

I can rub along without my watch and chain—
  Experience corroborates the boast;
And walk without a silver-headed cane;
  Subsist on plainer dinner than a roast;
I could learn to speak the language minus Bain,
  And even give up going to the play;
    I could part with many treasures,
    And some captivating pleasures—
But I couldn't do without my Pocket Gray.

3.

I could sacrifice the silly cigarette,
  And manage to exist without a pipe;
I could do without the fellows of my set—
  They're sometimes of an aggravating type;
I think I could forego without regret
Discussions on the value of the spray:
    But I might as well surrender
    My allowance— though it's slender—
As attempt to do without my Pocket Gray.

4.

Long after we have managed to get through,
  And started on professional careers,
We'll think upon this prompter and his cue,
  That helped us in the comedy for years.
Forgetful though we be of much we knew,
  We'll recollect this friendly little fay,
    For it lightened life and labour,
    This accommodating neighbour:
It were treason to forget the Pocket Gray.

THE CLINICAL EXAMINATION.

Words by John Smith, M.D., LL.D., etc.

Air–"Last May a braw wooer."
Arr. by J.K.L.

THE CLINICAL EXAMINATION.

I.

I was just aboot smoor'd wi' a kittlin' cough,
Whilk at times was a fair suffocation,
An' the sounds o' my voice were sae wheezin' an' rough,
I was thocht for till be in an ill situation,
Till be in an ill situation.

2.

I speired at my doctor gif ever I'd mend,
Whan he said 'twas his recommendation,
At the Royal Infirmary I suld attend
There tae mak o' my state a strong representation,
Tae mak a strong representation.

3.

They tell't me the place was braw buskit and new,
That for comforts it jist was perfection,
An' that I'd be attended by some bonnie doo,
Wha'd be there tae dae everything at my direction,
Dae onything at my direction.

4.

Sae I cam' to the yett in a cairt aman' straw,
An' was gaun tae commence my narration;
But afore I could speak I was whiskit awa',
As ye'll see for the purposes of illustration,
The purposes of illustration.

5.

The professor neist day cam' an' gied me a look,
An' at ance wi' profound admiration,
He clerkit me doon in a lang narrow book
As deservin' a clinical examination,
A clinical examination.

6.

I was proud at what seemed sic attention and care,
Till I fand to my great consternation,
That it meant I was fixed in a week, less or mair,
For experiments an' as a mode o' probation,
To serve as a kind o' probation.

7.

A curran o' callants wi' paper an' pens
Cam' in for their edification,
And the doctor sets ilk ane tae see if he kens
Whilken pairt o' my system's in maist perturbation,
Whilken pairt is in maist perturbation.

8.

They surrounded my bed, an' they pu'ed aff the claes,
Then glowered at my haill conformation;
An' inspeckit me a' frae the head to the taes,
In the first place tae see I had nae malformation,
Tae see I had nae malformation.

9.

They measured my stammick and knappit my skin,
An' speired gin I'd ony purgation;
Was I nervish, or deaf, or rheumatic, or blin',
Or whether my habits required reformation,
My habits required reformation.

10.

Ane said I was pushon't wi' owercome o' bile,
Some blethered o' degeneration;
Says a glib-gabbit loon whan I happened tae smile,
"He's deleerit, it's plain, an' needs incarceration,
It's plain he needs incarceration."

II.

My livers, my kidneys, my lungs, an' my heart
They disparaged without reservation;
'Deed they spak wi' contempt aboot every pairt
That exists in my bodily organisation,
My bodily organisation.

12.

They houpit my freens wad allow gin I dee'd,
A bit post-mortem examination,
For my thrapple in speerits they a' were agreed
Micht be useful tae show as a class-preparation,
Tae show as a class-preparation.

13.

Ilk threipit my case tae his mind was quite clear,—
Whilk tae me was but sma' consolation;
For they differed sae muckle it made it appear
I was ailin' o' everything in combination,
O' everything in combination.

14.

Then I rose frae my bed, an' I said I was cured,
For I felt that a continuation
O' the scandalous treatment that I had endured
Wad hae brocht a man's days till a quick termination,
My days till a swift termination.

15.

The doctors, the medicine, the nursing, the meat,
I maun aye haud in high estimation;
But I'd rather forgae them an' dee on my feet,
Than submit till a clinical examination,
A clinical examination.

THE EXAMINER'S SONG.

I.

I'm a 'Varsity examiner and Prof. who's wide awake,
Having studied student nature, I am up to every fake,
And can see through all their dodges, such as clerking with me twice,
Attending Drummond's meetings and then asking my advice.
I have intimate relations with the waster and the swot,
And when there's any spinning, I am always on the spot;
They may think they're very artful, and to scrape a pass may try,
But I've got my optic on 'em, and shall spin 'em by and by.
Chorus.　　They may bluff me, try to stuff me,
　　　　　But I've got 'em in my eye;
　　　　　And I'll spin 'em, yes, I'll spin 'em,
　　　　　I shall spin 'em by and by.

2.

There's a certain student fellow who does after lecture come,
With a tale of having suffered every woe in Christendom;
He has chronic Brights, he thinks, diabetes, pleurisy,
A sample of his tube-casts he has brought for me to see.
But, of course, there's nothing really wrong with him, you understand,
He only wants to know me, so this little fake he's planned,
As he thinks if I examine him, I'll let him through it fly,
But I merely wink the other eye, and spin him by and by. *Chorus.*

3.

There are students that I know of, who are eminent "boozees",
Who, when they get a cheque with which to pay their lawful fees,
Do immediately go on the razzle dazzle (or the loose,)
Thus sending Profs. and fees alike to—well, let's say the dooce!
Then they come to me and tell me that the mails have gone astray,
And would it be convenient at the session's end to pay?
It's a case of nolens volens, so of course I have to try
Just to whistle for my fee, but I shall spin 'em by and by. *Chorus.*

4.

There's the man who takes the medals on the extra-mural side,
And the man who scamps my lectures, and who does a festive slide,
And who yet in some mysterious way gets cards in, twenty-six;
To count them for him makes me kick, like Paul, against the pricks;
There's the man who shouts derisively, and loudly laughs, Ho, Ho!
When I'm desirous most to make my annual jokelet go;
There's the man who carves his name upon the gallery-benches high;
I am keeping them blue papers, and shall spin 'em by and by. *Chorus.*

THE EXAMINER'S SONG.

Words by Dr. R. J. A. Berry.

Music *from "Faust up to Date",
by Meyer Lutz.

I'm a 'Var-si-ty ex-am-in-er and Prof. who's wide a-wake, Hav-ing stud-ied stud-ent na-ture, I am up to ev-'ry fake, And can see thro' all their dod-ges, such as clerk-ing with me twice, At-tend-ing Drummond's meet-ings and then ask-ing my ad-vice. I have in-ti-mate re-

* Printed by arrangement with Messrs. E. Ascherberg & Co, 16 Mortimer Street, London, W.

la - tions with the was - ter and the swot, And when there's a - ny

spin - ning, I am al - ways on the spot; They may think they're ve - ry

art - ful, and to scrape a pass may try, But I've got my op - tic on 'em, and shall

spin 'em by and by. They may bluff me, try to stuff me, But I've got 'em in my

eye; And I'll spin 'em, yes, I'll spin 'em, I shall spin 'em by and by.

CHORUS.

They may bluff me, try to stuff me, But I've got 'em in my eye; And I'll spin 'em, yes, I'll spin 'em, I shall spin 'em by and by.

GIVE A FEE.

(A song for young Advocates.)

Words by John Stuart Blackie. (1834.)

Air "Buy a Broom".
Arr by J. K. L.

I. O listen, of Scotch and of Civil Law Doctors all, So - li - ci - tors, A - gents, Ac - count - ants, to me; O listen, of strifes and of law - suit con - coctors all, And give to a

poor starv-ing law-yer a fee. Give a fee,

SPOKEN.

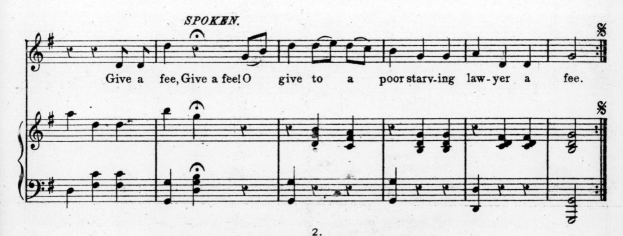

Give a fee, Give a fee! O give to a poor starv-ing law-yer a fee.

2.

The soldier and sailor they dash on and splash on,
    And, sure of their pay, scour the land and the sea;
But we peak and pine here, and long, long years pass on,
    Before our eyes blink at our first guinea fee.
        Give a fee, etc.

3.

The Church is an Eden of violets and roses,
    The Bishop its Adam, from drudgery free;
The big burly priest on his soft down reposes,
    While we must still fag on, and cry, "Give a fee!"
        Give a fee, etc.

4.

The quack he sells wholesale his pills universal,
    And straight waxes richer than sagest M. D.;
But we still must con o'er the same dull rehearsal,
    And leave one or two old stagers to pocket the fee.
        Give a fee, etc.

5.

Here sit I, all frozen; my youth's glowing visions,
    See-saw like a Chinese joss or a Turkish Cadi;
I seek for no learning beyond the decisions,
    And my soul's proud ideal is a bright guinea fee.
        Give a fee, Give a fee!
        O force me no longer to cry, "Give a fee."

SAM'EL SUMPH.

Words by Prof. John Stuart Blackie.

Adapted to Sir Herbert Oakeley's arrangement*
of the Music of "Duncan Gray."

In "Eighteen Scottish Melodies arranged, for Male Chorus, for the Universities of Scotland", and orchestrated for Edinburgh University Musical Society, by Sir Herbert Oakeley.

Greek-ing o't!

2.

Latin Syntax vexed him sore,
  When he tried the Greeking o't,
For Cæsar stands at Homer's door
  When folks try the Greeking o't.
Quod and *ut* he understood,
At "speech direct" they called him good,
But *qui* with the subjunctive mood
  Was the crook in the lot at the Greeking o't!

3.

One thing truth commands to tell,
  Ha, ha, the Greeking o't!
English he could hardly spell,
  But what's that to the Greeking o't!
English fits the vulgar clan,
The buying and the selling man,
But for the learn'd the only plan
  Is a close grip at the Greeking o't.

4.

How he wandered through the verb,
  It pains my tongue the speaking o't,
He said it was a bitter herb,
  When he tried the Greeking o't.
Wi' mony a wrench and mony a screw,
At last he warstled bravely through,
All except a tense or two,
  When he tried the Greeking o't!

5.

How he fared with ἠ and ἂν
  When he tried the Greeking o't,
Δἠ and γε, and all their clan,
  It's weel worth the speaking o't.
These feckless dots of words, quo' he,
That are nae bigger than a flea,
We'll skip them ow'r and let them be,—
  They'll nae be missed at the Greeking o't!

6.

A' the story for to tell,
  Were nae end to the speaking o't,
But this thing in the end befell,
  When he tried the Greeking o't;
Though his heart was free frae vice
(Men are sometimes trapped like mice),
They plucked him ance, they plucked him twice,
  When he tried the Greeking o't!

7.

Sair cast doun was learned Sam
  At this end o' the Greeking o't;
He could dae nae mair wi' cram
  At this stage o' the Greeking o't.
But he was teugh as ony Scot,
He was plucked, but yield would not,
Sooner would he hang and rot,
  Than thus be balked at the Greeking o't!

8.

At the door he made a din,
  Rap, rap, for the Greeking o't!
Is the Greek Professor in?
  Yes, yes, for the Greeking o't!
Sam his plea wi' tears would win,
He fleeched and grat his een quite blin',
To pluck him twice was just a sin,
  For a sma' fault at the Greeking o't!

9.

Professor was a kindly man,
  Ha, ha, the Greeking o't!
Felt for a' the student clan
  That swat sair at the Greeking o't,
"Though you're nae just in the van,
My heart is wae your worth to ban;
Ye hae done the best ye can,
  So ye may pass at the Greeking o't."

10.

Sam'el Sumph is now M. A.,
  Ha, ha, for the Greeking o't!
He can preach and he can pray,—
  That's the fruit of the Greeking o't.
He can thunder loud and fell,
An awfu' power in him doth dwell,
To ope and shut the gates of hell,—
  That's the prize o' the Greeking o't.

11.

Wait a year and ye will see,
  Ha, ha, the Greeking o't!
High upon the tap o' the tree,
  Sam perch'd by the Greeking o't!
In the Kirk Assembly he
Sits as big as big can be,
Moderator Sam, D. D.,
  That's the crown o' the Greeking o't!

A MATHEMATIC MONODY.

Words by John Malcolm Bulloch.

Music by Ernest Newton.

Andante moderato.

Allegro mod^{to}.

1. De-void of mathe-ma-tic brain, I puzzle o-ver x and y; Dull propos-i-tions are a pain, I nev-er yet di-gest-ed π, 'Twere hard to give the rea-son why, But Maths have always been my thorn, And thus I nev-er cease to cry- "Ah, why was Eu-clid ev - er born?" Some

Andante moderato.

luck-y birds were made to fly, And some the low-ly earth a - dorn; They

mere-ly wad-dle, such as I: "Ah, why was Eu-clid ev - er born?" Some

luck-y birds were made to fly, And some the low-ly earth a - dorn; They

mere-ly waddle, such as I: "Ah, why was Euclid ev - er born?" born?"

2.
I don't object to Dr. Bain,
  Or Mr. Mill, although he's dry;
I'm docile under Hegel's rein,
  And into Ego love to pry;
I know the shades of δε and και;
  But then my heart is rudely torn
By props. and problems that I try –
  "Ah, why was Euclid ever born?" *Chorus.*

3.
It is not that I am inane,
  I'm not an intellectual guy;
And yet I study Maths. in vain,
  And shall, in vain, until I die.
I've tried to work when night is nigh,
  And turned again at early morn.
It's useless: I am forced to sigh,
  "Ah, why was Euclid ever born?" *Chorus.*

THE STUDENT AND HIS BOW-WOW.

Words by John Malcolm Bulloch.

*Music by Joseph Tabrar.

1. When some fel-lows leave a
2. You might think the Quad. a

mo - ther, And a mo-ther's a-pron string, They have scarce the grace to
ken - nel If you saw it now and then, When the a - ca - de - mic

smo - ther Their re - solve to have a fling; For they hold the old tra -
Phe - nyl Strolls to col - lege af - ter ten; At his heels a sa - ble

* Printed by arrangement with Messrs. Francis, Day, & Hunter, 195 Oxford Street, London, W.

di - tion That a youth must be a romp, When he joins that com-pe-
col - lie, While a bull is on the chain: For the own-er thinks it's

f Chorus in unison.

ti - tion, Which we al-ways call "The Comp." They say they're not complete without a
jol - ly. To be dog-gy on the brain. If you want to cut a dash, Get a

f 8va higher 2nd time.

bow-wow, bow-wow, At their pa-tent-lea-ther'd feet, Runs a bow-wow, bow-wow, They
bow-wow, bow-wow, Though you pos-si-bly may smash, I'll al-low-wow, low-wow, And you

think an ug - ly bull, Is a start to play the fool, And they'll
may be pack'd a - way, To New Zea - land or Ca - thay, To a

1.
set it on a meou, wow, wow, wow, wow, wow.

2.
sho - vel or a plow, wow, wow, wow, wow, wow, wow.

THE PIPE.

Taken from the Toronto University Song Book, and printed by permission of I. Suckling & Sons of Toronto, Canada, and Chappell & Co., 50 New Bond Street, London, England.

worst wars cease in a pipe of peace, Which soothes the nerves of sor - row.

CHORUS. *Accompaniment same as for first eight bars of Solo.*

Then hur - rah for the pipe so rich and ripe, With its am - ber mouth so yel - low, And the curl-ing smoke that doth e - voke A fra-grance mild and mel - low.

2.

Let philosophers rant of Fichte and Kant,
   Of Hartley and his vibrations,
And puzzle their wits with Clarke, Leibnitz,
   Time, space, and their relations;
Yet six feet space will end their race,
   And prove their sciences trashes,
While Time with a wipe will break their pipe,
   And Death knock out the ashes. *Chorus.*

3.

Let the soldier boast of the mighty host,
   Of the pride and the pomp of battle,
Of the war-steed's bound, and the clarion's sound,
   And the cannon's thundering rattle;
Yet there's more delight with a friend at night,
   And a song and a pipe also,
Than in balls and bombs, and fifes and drums,
   And military show. *Chorus.*

POPE AND SULTAN.

Translation by Charles Lever.

Con spirito.

Second tenors to accentuate melody.

1. *Der Papst lebt herr-lich in der Welt, in der Welt, Er lebt von sei-nem Ab-lass-*
1. The Pope, he leads a hap-py life; hap-py life; He fears not married care nor

geld, Ab-lassgeld, Er trinkt den al-ler-be-sten Wein; Ich möchte doch der Papst auch
strife, care nor strife, He drinks the best of Rhenish wine, I would the Pope's gay lot were

den be-sten Wein,
of Rhenish wine;

sein, Er trinkt den al-ler-be-sten Wein; Ich möchte doch der Papst auch sein.
mine, He drinks the best of Rhenish wine; I would the Pope's gay lot were mine.

den be-sten Wein;
of Rhenish wine;

2.	**2.**
Doch nein, er ist ein armer Wicht,	But then all happy's not his life—
Ein holdes Mädchen küsst ihn nicht,	He has not maid, nor blooming wife;
Er schläft in seinem Bett allein;	Nor child has he to raise his hope—
Ich möchte doch der Papst nicht sein.	I would not wish to be the Pope.
3.	**3.**
Der Sultan lebt in Saus und Braus,	The Sultan better pleases me,
Er wohnt in einem grossen Haus	His is a life of jollity;
Voll wunderschöner Mägdelein;	His wives are many as he will—
Ich möchte doch auch Sultan sein.	I would the Sultan's throne then fill.
4.	**4.**
Doch nein, er ist ein armer Mann,	But even he's a wretched man;
Er lebt nach seinem Alkoran,	He must obey his Al-Koran,
Er trinkt nicht einen Tropfen Wein;	And dares not drink one drop of wine—
Ich möchte doch nicht Sultan sein.	I would not change his lot for mine.
5.	**5.**
Getrennt wünscht' ich mir beider Glück	So then I'll hold my lowly stand,
Nicht einen einz'gen Augenblick,	And live in German Vaterland;
Doch das ging' ich mit Freuden ein:	I'll kiss my maiden fair and fine,
Bald Papst, bald Sultan möcht' ich sein.	And drink the best of Rhenish wine.
6.	**6.**
Drum, Mädchen, gieb mir einen Kuss,	Whene'er my maiden kisses me,
Denn jetzt bin ich der Sultanus;	I'll think that I the Sultan be;
Drum, traute Brüder, schenkt mir ein,	And when my cheery glass I tope,
Damit ich auch der Papst kann sein.	I'll fancy then I am the Pope.

THE COLLEGE GOWN.

Words by Rev. J. Campbell.*   Air_"Pope. and Sultan".

I.

Oft in the classic page I've read
  Of Graces three and Muses nine,
And many a time with aching head
  I've begged them to suggest a line.
Now heathen dames I bid depart,
  And her my Grace, my Muse, I own,—
She shall inspire the poet's heart—
  She mended my old College Gown.

2.

Dynamic forces ne'er can move
  Th' ecstatic zero of my soul,
No calculus compute its love,
  Nor optic powers discern the whole.
Though squared and cubed, no lapse of years
  Can e'er her fond remembrance drown,
Nay, though they numbered thrice the tears
  She mended in my College Gown.

3.

No language can express her charms,
  No living tongue her virtues tell;
Her name the poet's pen disarms,
  And dares his powers to break the spell.
Nor would he, if he could, disclose
  That name in every language known;
'Tis stated best in English prose—
  She mended my old College Gown.

4.

Philosophy perchance may please
  The earnest and enquiring mind,
But neither mighty Socrates
  Nor Cicero himself could find
A secret that in ages past
  Baffled sages of renown:
The *summum bonum* found at last!
  She mended my old College Gown.

5.

Great wonders Science brings to light,
  Great truths her growing powers unfold,
And Nature spreads before our sight
  A thousand beauties new and old.
Yet one o'er all I still prefer,
  Who in her kingdom wears the crown;
The world were empty wanting her
  Who mended my old College Gown.

* Taken from the University of Toronto Song Book, and printed by permission of I. Suckling & Sons of Toronto, Canada, and Chappell & Co., 50 New Bond Street, London, England.

RE-UNITED.

I.

We are students by nature, and students by name,
And we study to climb the long ladder of fame,
But now from the trammels of study we're free,
And we'll be as jolly as jolly can be!
Chorus.   Then fill up your glasses and fill them up well,
        Let Bacchus for once have a chance with his spell;
        And fill up your pipes and let the smoke free,
        And all be as jolly as jolly can be!

2.

There are some of us here in the medical line,
In the footsteps of Lister aspiring to shine,
And with diligence therefore we pore over Quain,
But we cannot for ever o'er forceps remain. *Chorus.*

3.

Away with the doctrines philosophy owns;
We promptly dismiss them to follow the bones;
And to-night young divines more human must feel;
To-morrow they'll follow the path of Mc Neill. *Chorus.*

4.

There are some with a leaning to science inclined—
Let them leave all their arcs and triangles behind,
And the limit of X to infinity send,
While the students of Nature would hail them as friend. *Chorus.*

5.

There are others here present who pleasure would seek
In reading the loves of a Roman or Greek,
But forget for the nonce all these wonderful tales;
Here the story of Bacchus and Baccy prevails. *Chorus.*

6.

Then of course there are students who study the Law,
And wear out their boots in the Parliament Ha'_
If of future Lord President's gown they would dream,
In a halo of smoke let them perfect their scheme. *Chorus.*

7.

The Tory and Liberal here must agree
Re-union to hold, and in unity be,
And the only coercion of which we approve
Is to drink to our Union and laggards remove. *Chorus.*

8.

Now, my friends, on this joyous occasion, we'll sing,
And with merriment hearty will make the roof ring;
And we all will unite till our pipes cease to draw,
To puff and to taste, in obedience to law.
Chorus.   So fill up your glasses and fill them up well,
        Let Bacchus for once have a chance with his spell;
        And fill up your pipes and let the smoke free,
        For we'll all be as jolly as jolly should be!

RE-UNITED.

Words by A.P. Melville.

Air, "Bonnie Dundee."
Arr. by J.K.L.

1. We are stu - dents by na - ture and stu - dents by name, And we
2. There are some of us here in the 'me - di - cal line, In the
3. A - way with the doc - trines phi - lo - so - phy owns; We

stu - dy to climb the long lad - der of fame; But now from the tram - mels of
foot - steps of Lis - ter as - pir - ing to shine, And with di - li - gence there - fore we
promptly dis - miss them to fol - low the bones; And to - night young di - vines more

stu - dy we're free, And we'll be as jol - ly as jol - ly can be!
pore o - ver Quain, But we can - not for ev - er o'er for - ceps re - main.
hu - man must feel; To - mor - row they'll fol - low the path of Mc - Neill.

CHORUS.

Then fill up your glas - ses and fill them up well, Let

Bac - chus for once have a chance with his spell; And fill up your pipes and

let the smoke free, And all be as jol - ly as jol - ly can be!

rall.

TRIFOLIUM.

Song of the Wandering Students
of the Middle Ages.

Music by J. J. Flemming.
Arr. for 3 voices by W. H. M.

Andante.

Dul-ce cum so- da-li-bus Sa-pit vi-num bo- num. Os-cu-la-ri vir-gi-nes
In me Bac-chus ex-ci-tat Ve-ne-ris a- mo-rem; Ve-nus mox po- e-ti-cum
Si ty-ran-nus ju-be-at: "Vi-num da-to!" da- rem. "Non a-ma-to vir-gi-nes!"

Dul-ci-us est do- num; Do-num est dul- cis-si-mum Ly-ra ceu Ma- ro- num;
Phœ-bi dat fu- ro- rem; Im-mor-ta-lem Phœ-bus dux Com-pa-rat ho- no- rem;
Ae-gre non a- ma-rem. "Fran-ge ly-ram, ab-ji-ce!" Per-ti-nax ne- ga- rem!

Si his tri-bus gau-de- am, Sper-no re-gis thro- num.
Vae mi-hi, si tri-bus his In-fi-de-lis fo- rem!
"Ly-ram da, seu mo-re- rel" Can-tans ex-spi- ra- rem.

BRÜDER, LAGERT EUCH IM KREISE.

Brothers, circle round in chorus.

Student-Song of the 18th century.
Translation by Prof. John Stuart Blackie. (1841.)

Melody from J. G. W. Schneider's
"Commers-Liedern". (1801.)

Allegro maestoso.

BRÜDER, LAGERT EUCH IM KREISE.
(Brothers, circle round in chorus.)

Student-Song of the 18th century.
Translation by Prof. John Stuart Blackie. (1841.)

Melody from J. G. W. Schneider's
"Commers Liedern". (1801.)

1.

Brüder, lagert euch im Kreise,
Trinkt nach alter Väter Weise,
Leert die Gläser, schwenkt die Hüte,
Auf der gold'nen Freiheit Wohl!

I.

Brothers, circle round in chorus,
Sing as sang our sires before us,
Quaff your glasses, wave your bonnets,
To our glorious liberty!

2.

Flur, wo wir als Knaben spielten,
Ahnung künft'ger Thaten fühlten,
Süsser Traum der Kinderjahre
Kehr' noch einmal uns zurück!

2.

Paths by rosy boyhood haunted,
When young hearts with high hopes panted,
To each early fond remembrance
Fill a brimming glass of glee!

3.

Mädchen, die mit keuschen Trieben
Nur den braven Burschen lieben,
Nie der Tugend Reiz entstellen,
Sei ein schäumend Glas gebracht!

3.

To all lovely maidens fill we!
Chaste as charming may they still be!
Pour a sparkling bright libation_
To all maidens now drink we!

4.

Deutschlands Jünglingen zu Ehren
Will auch ich mein Gläschen leeren,
Die für Ehr' und Freiheit fechten;
Selbst ihr Fall sei heilig mir!

4.

To our country's sons who love her,
Fill a bumper flowing over,
Men who stand and fall for freedom,
Fatherland, who fell for thee!

5.

Männern, die das Herz uns rühren,
Uns den Pfad der Weisheit führen,
Deren Beispiel wir verehren
Sei ein dreifach Hoch gebracht!

5.

Men who moved our hearts to duty,
Taught us wisdom, showed us beauty,
Whom we honour, whom we follow,
Fill to them with three times three!

6.

Brüdern, die vor vielen Jahren
Unsers Bundes Glieder waren,
Die der Bund stets liebt und ehret
Sei ein schäumend Glas geweiht!

6.

Friends, whom Fate from friends hath riven,
To hot suns and cold skies driven,
Far from home new homes creating,
Bless them, God, where'er they be!

7.

Brüdern, die befreit von Kummer,
Ruh'n den langen Grabesschlummer,
Weih'n wir, der Erinn'rung heilig,
Diese frohe Libation.

7.

Brothers, whom no sorrows cumber,
Cradled in death's dewy slumber,
Pour to them this pure libation_
May they sleep, and dream of us!

8.

Unter'm Schatten heil'ger Linden
Werden wir uns wiederfinden,
Wo sich Brüder froh umarmen
In dem Hain Elysiums.

8.

And, when life's harsh toils are over,
Under lime-trees' cooling cover,
Brother brave shall meet brave brother,
And remain for ever thus.

9.

Wenn ich deinen Kahn besteige
Trauter Charon, O, dann reiche
Noch einmal den Labebecher
Mir für meinen Obolus!

9.

When I cross the dingy ferry,
Trusty Charon, in thy wherry,
O then, one last draught restoring
Give for my last obolus!

A CHEQUER'D CAREER.

Words by Dr. David Rorie.

Air—"Oh, dear! What can the matter be?" 18th Century.

1. When I first was a *civis* I studied Humanity,
Cos and *Sine* show'd me Life's utter inanity,
He-gel and Kant prov'd that all things were vanity,
All save a che-quer'd ca-reer!

2. So I next had a shy at what men call Divinity;
That sort of thing for me had no af-finity,
B. D. I left for who chose to go win it, I
kept on my che-quer'd ca-reer!

3. Behold me now one of the Fac-ul-ty Legal And
learn-ing the Sci-ence of trick and in-vei-gle, But
in it there's more of the vul-ture than ea-gle—Much
bet-ter a che-quer'd ca-reer!

4.

At note-book and pencil by no means a raw-bones,
I landed at last in the midst of the Sawbones;
Through hosts of smashed legs and excised upper jaw-bones
 I kept on my chequered career! *Chorus.*

5.

In dreams I oft wonder what next I may chance to be —
Fiji Prime Minister? Marshal of France to be?
Bashi Bazouk with a ten-foot-eight lance to be?
 Still on my chequered **career!** *Chorus.*

THE DARWINIAN THEORY.

I.

Oh! have you heard the news of late,
About our great original state?
If you have not, I will relate
  The grand Darwinian theory.
Take care as you saunter along the street,
How you tread on the dust beneath your feet:
You may crush a cherub in embryo sweet,
For each atom may hold a germ complete,
Which, by some mystical process slow,
And selective power, to a monkey may grow,
And from that to a man, the truth to show
  Of the grand Darwinian theory.

2.

The beginning of all was a little cell,
Composed of what substance no one can tell,
Endowed with a power to develop and swell
  Into general life by this theory.
With a power to select what it wished to be_
A fungus or flower, a bush or a tree,
A fowl of the air, or a fish of the sea,
A cow or a sheep, a bug or a flea,
Or, if tired of these, it may change its plan:
Be a cat or a dog, or O-rang-oo-tan,
But culminating at last in a man
  By this grand Darwinian theory.

3.

Your attention, ladies_ let me win it;
Just think of this theory for a minute;
Is there really not something distressing in it_
  To think that you sprang from a monkey?
That delicate hand was a monkey's paw,
Those lovely lips graced a monkey's jaw,
Those handsome ankles, so trim and neat,
One time surmounted a monkey's feet;
Those sparkling eyes a monkey did lend,
That graceful form from one did descend,
From a monkey you borrowed the Grecian bend,
  By this grand Darwinian theory.

4.

Such murderers we_ far worse than Cain,
For darker deeds our characters stain;
For thousands of brothers we've eaten and slain,
  By the grand Darwinian theory.
When sitting at breakfast, and picking the wing
Of a pigeon, or grouse, or of some other thing;
Or dining on mutton_ or lamb, if in spring;
Or on salmon, or trout, or on cod, or on ling_
Gaze into the future, and say, can't you see
What horrible cannibals we must be,
Devouring the flesh, which may yet become we,
  By the grand Darwinian theory?

5.

But why should the theory end with man?
If he has been less, surely more he can,
And should be, by the great developing plan
  Of the grand Darwinian theory.
Why should he not on this earth yet be,
An angel, or god, like Mercury,
With a wing on each shoulder, each ankle and knee?
Oh! how delightful then it will be,
When sighing and wishing your sweetheart to see,
To wipe your beak, and just upwards flee,
Like birds_ and meet your love on a tree,
  On the top of a hill, by this theory.

THE DARWINIAN THEORY.

Words by John Young, C.E.

Air, "The King of the Cannibal Islands."

Allegretto.

1. Oh! have you heard the news of late, A-bout our great o-ri-gi-nal state? If you have not, I will re-late The grand Darwin-i-an theo-ry. Take care as you saunter a-long the street, How you tread on the dust be-neath your feet: You may crush a che-rub in em-bry-o sweet, For each a-tom may hold a germ complete, Which, by some mys-ti-cal pro-cess slow, And se-lec-tive pow'r, to a monkey may grow, And from that to a man, the truth to show Of the grand Darwin-i-an theo-ry.

CHORUS.

1. Oh! ho - key, po - key, Kan - yuwan, From nothing to something, from monkey to man. Oh!
2. Oh! ho - key, po - key, pow'r of se - lec - tion, Choose your self your par - ti - cu - lar section: A
3. Oh! ho - key, po - key, pro - toplasm, Tween monkeys and men there is no chasm; Why

this is the great de - vel - op - ing plan, Of the grand Dar - win - i - an theo - ry.
peas - ant, or lord with a great con - nec - tion: By the grand Dar - win - i - an theo - ry.
should - n't you clasp them to your bo - som? They're in - fant men by this theo - ry.

4.

Oh! hokey, pokey, ringo - ging,
The cannibal islands once had a King
Who ate his own kin; but to us he's no - thing,
When compared in the light of this theory.

5.

Oh! hokey, pokey, ringo - ging,
The world then literally on the wing,
No street cabs needed, or any such thing,
By the grand Darwinian theory.

AMO, AMAS, I LOVE A LASS.

Words by Dr. Arnold.

Air—"The Mouse and the Frog."

Moderato.

1. A-mo, A-mas, I love a lass, As a ce-dar tall and slen-der; Sweet cowslip's grace is her no-min-a-tive case, And she's of the fe-mi-nine gen-der.

2. Oh, how Bel-la, my pu-el-la, I'll kiss se-cu-la se-cu-lo-rum. If I've luck, sir, she's my ux-or, O di-es be-ne-dic-to-rum!

CHORUS.

Ro-rum, Co-rum, sunt di-vo-rum, Ha-rum, sca-rum di-vo; Tag rag, mer-ry der-ry per-i-wig and hat-band Hic hoc ho-rum ge-ni-ti-vo!

D. S.

THE STUDENT SONG.

Words by Robert L. Bremner.

Music by W. Henry Maxfield.

1. Hail to thee, Song of the care-less col-le-gians!
2. Know you the boat songs of Ca-na-da's prai-rie land?
3. Song of first man-hood, so-no-rous roof-sun-de-rer,
4. Come, then, ye days of good luck or ad-ver-si-ty!

Hail to thy tu-mult of re-so-nant chords!
Know you the song of the brown gon-do-lier?
How thy loud e-cho ex-ul-ted and died!
Who knows the lot in the lap of his fate?

Deep as the war-cry of Vik-ing Nor-we-gians,
Fear-less we chal-lenge you: Tell to us where a land
Rose yet a-gain like the shout of the Thun-de-rer,
Days may be-fall when good friends are in scar-ci-ty;

Clear as the clash of their good - ly broad - swords,
Rings with a cho - rus so stir - ring and clear?
Swelled like the Rhine - land's broad Alp - fos - tered tide,
Love may swing light in the ba - lance with hate;

Loud as the Hunt - call through O - din's vast re - gions,
Nor can you match in the mu - sic of Fai - ry - land,
Swept like the horse of a Lid - des - dale plun - de - rer,
Raise we the chants of our old U - ni - ver - si - ty,

} Speeding a - long,

colla voce

Ra - pid and strong, The glo - ri - ous sound of a Stu - dent Song.

CHORUS.

Speed - ing a - long, Ra - pid and strong, The glo - ri - ous sound of a Stu - dent Song.

D. S. al Segna.

OUR NOBLE SELVES.

Words by John Malcolm Bulloch.

Music by Ernest Newton.

pos - si - bly our ri - vals may a - mass   More   know-ledge than the Col - lege By the

cres.

Dee,   But   none of them can pos-si-bly sur - pass   Our   weather and our heather And our

f   *rall.*

sea,   Our   wea-ther and our hea-ther And our   sea.   sea.

2.

If you study at St. Thomas's or Bart's,
    You have to breathe an atmosphere of fog;
The Proctor inconsiderately parts
    The easy-going student from his dog;
There is wondrous fascination (they aver)
      To shiver as a river—
         Devotee:
But as for me, I'd any day prefer
      Our weather and our heather
         And our sea.

3.

Now Manchester may beat us in the race
    Of science and of laboratory lore;
And Birmingham (though scarce a pretty place)
    In teaching modern languages may score;
Again, we hear of gallant little Wales,
      Of Jena, and Vienna,
         And "Paree":
But then we weigh against them in the scales
      Our weather and our heather
         And our sea.

CAPPED AND DOCTORED AND A'.

I.

I yince was a light-headed laddie,
  A dreamin' an' daunderin' loon,
Just escap'd from the rod o' my daddie,
  And the skirts o' my mither's broun goun.
But now I cut loftier capers
  An' the beer that I drink is na' sma',
When I see my ain name in the papers,
  Capped and doctored and a'.

2.

My parish I wadna besmutch
  Wi' words that look heartless and hard,
But I knew there of life just as much,
  As a hen in the farmer's kail yard.
I got a good tailor to suit me,
  My feet were richt decently shod;
But the smell o' the peat was about me,
  And my manners were awkward and odd!

3.

Frae the school I came up to the College,
  As a calf comes up to a cow;
Wi' a wonderful thirst for all knowledge,
  And scraps of learning a few!
Through Virgil I stoutly could hammer,
  A book, or it may be twa;
And Greek, just a taste o' the grammar,
  To look better than naething ava!

4.

A wonderful place is the College;
  I felt like a worm getting wings,
When I heard the great mill-wheel of knowledge
  Turn round with all possible things!
A marvellous place is the College;
  Professor's a marvellous man,
To find for such mountains of knowledge
  Such room in a single brain-pan!

5.

All races and peoples and nations
  Were lodged in that wonderful brain;
Proud systems and big speculations,
  All possible things to explain.
All creatures at various stages,
  From mollusc and monkey to man,
Through millions of billions of ages,
  That make up life's wonderful plan!

6.

I confess I was glamoured at first —
  Looked round wi' a stupid surprise;
But from session to session there burst
  New light on my widening eyes:
I could talk of attraction and force,
  Of motion and mind and matter:
And thought it a thing quite of course,
  When phosphorus burned in water.

7.

My logic is lithe as an eel,
  My philosophy deep as a well;
My rhetoric spins like a wheel,
  My Greek, for a Scot, pretty well.
Of my Bible I know quite enough,
  Not, like Chalmers, to preach and to pray,
But to give a glib foel a rebuff,
  And to keep the black devil at bay!

8.

You may ca' me a lean, lanky student,
  A chicken new out o' the shell;
But with time, if I'm patient and prudent,
  I may be Professor mysel'.
My head with citations well stocket,
  I may sit in the chair at my ease,
With a thousand a year in my pocket,
  And six months to do what I please.

9.

Then fill your glasses, my boys,
  Let mirth and jollity sway!
'Tis fit with my friends to rejoice,
  When I'm Capped and Doctored to-day!
This night may not stupidly pass
  With beer, or coffee, or tea;
But of champagne a bright sparkling glass
  Shall foam to my noble degree!

CAPPED AND DOCTORED AND A'.

Words by Prof. John Stuart Blackie.

Air – "Woo'd and Married and a'."
Arr. by J. K. L.

1. I yince was a light-head-ed lad-die, A dream-in' an' daun-der-in' loon, Just e-scap'd from the rod o' my dad-die, And the skirts o' my mi-ther's broun goun. But now I cut lof-ti-er ca-pers, An' the beer that I drink is na' sma', When I see my ain name in the pa-pers, Capped and doc-tored and a'.

CHORUS.

1. Capped and Doc - tored and a', Doc - tored and Capped and a'! Right
2. Capped and Doc - tored and a', Doc - tored and Capped and a'! I'm as
3. Capped and Doc - tored and a', Doc - tored and Capped and a'! I'm as

sure 'tis a beau - ti - ful thing To be Capped and Doc - tored and a'!
proud as a Pope or a King, To be Capped and Doc - tored and a'!
proud as a Pope or a King, To be Capped and Doc - tored and a'!

4.

Capped and Doctored and a'!
Doctored and Capped and a'!
I feel like a bird on the wing,
When I'm Capped and Doctored and a'!

5.

Capped and Doctored and a'!
Doctored and Capped and a'!
It gives one a wonderful swing
To be Capped and Doctored and a'.

6.

Capped and Doctored and a'!
Doctored and Capped and a'!
The lad has the genuine ring
Who is Capped and Doctored and a'.

7.

Capped and Doctored and a'!
Doctored and Capped and a'!
I leap and I dance and I sing,
Now Capped and Doctored and a'!

8.

I'll know how to find my own place
In the world, with great and with sma';
And I'll no be the last in the race,
Being Capped and Doctored and a'!

9.

Brim your glasses, my boys!
In the Church, or it may be the law,
Tom Tidy will yet make a noise,
Being Capped and Doctored and a'!

SONGS OF THE NATIONS.

*"That man's the best Cosmopolite
Who loves his native country best."*

TENNYSON,   *Hands all round.*

GOD SAVE THE KING.

Maestoso.

Ascribed to Henry Carey. (1743.)

SCOTS, WHA HAE WI' WALLACE BLED.

Words by Robert Burns. (1793.)

Arr. by Sir Herbert Oakeley, Mus., Doc., etc.

* This song may be taken with advantage half a tone higher, in B♮.
From "Eighteen Scottish Melodies arranged for Male Chorus, for the Universities of Scotland", and Orchestrated for Edinburgh University Musical Society, by Sir Herbert Oakeley. Printed by his kind permission.

RULE, BRITANNIA.

Words by James Thomson. (1700-48.)

Melody by Dr. Arne. (1740.)
Arr. for male voices by W. H. M.

1. char - ter of the land, And guard-ian an — gels sang the strain.
2. flour-ish great and free, The dread and en — vy of them all.
3. match-less beau - ty crown'd, And man - ly heart to guard the fair.

Ped.   *

FULL CHORUS.

Rule, Bri - tan - nia! Bri - tan - nia rule the waves;

ff

Ped.   *

Bri - tons nev — — er shall be slaves.

rall.

Ped.   *Ped.*   *Ped.*

BRITANNIA, THE PRIDE OF THE OCEAN.

The Red, White and Blue.

Arr. by J. K. L.

Maestoso.

1. Bri - tan - nia, the pride of the o-cean, The home of the brave and the
2. When war spread its wide des - o - la-tion, And threat-en'd our land to de -

free, The shrine of the sai - lor's de - votion, No land can com-pare un - to
form, The ark then of free-dom's foun - dation, Bri - tan-nia rode safe thro' the

thee. Thy man-dates make he - roes as - sem-ble, With vic'try's bright lau-rels in
storm; With her gar-lands of vic - t'ry a - round her, When so no - bly she bore her brave

view, Thy banners make ty-ran-ny trem-ble, When borne by the Red, White and Blue.
crew, With her flag float-ing proud-ly be - fore her, The boast of the Red, White and Blue.

rall.

CHORUS.

When borne by the Red, White and Blue,
The boast of the Red, White and Blue,

When borne by the Red, White and
The boast of the Red, White and

Blue, Thy banners make tyran-ny tremble,
Blue, With her flag float-ing proud-ly be-fore her,

When borne by the Red, White and
The boast of the Red, White and

Blue.
Blue.

THE WEARING OF THE GREEN.

Irish Street Ballad, (1798.)

Old English Melody.

1. Oh! Pad - dy dear, and did you hear the news that's go - ing round? The
2. Then since the col - our we must wear is Eng - land's cru - el red, 'Twill

sham - rock is for - bid by law to grow on I - rish ground; Saint
serve but to re - mind us of the blood that has been shed; You may

Pat - rick's day no more we'll keep, his col - our can't be seen, For
take the sham - rock from your hat and cast it on the sod, But

there's a cru - el law a - gin the wear - ing of the green. I
nev - er fear, 'twill take root there, tho' un - der foot 'tis trod. When

MEN OF HARLECH.

* Words by William Duthie.

Allegro marziale.

Welsh Melody. Arr. for male voices by W. H. M.

1. Men of Har-lech! in the hol-low, Do ye hear, like rush-ing bil-low,
2. Rock-y steeps and pas-ses nar-row, Flash with spear and flight of ar-row;

Wave on wave that surg-ing fol-low Bat-tle's dis-tant sound?'Tis the tramp of Sax-on foe-men,
Who would think of death or sor-row?Death is glo-ry now! Hurl the reel-ing horse-men o-ver!

Sax-on spear-men, Sax-on bow-men; Be they knights, or hinds, or yeomen,They shall bite the ground!
Let the earth dead foe-men cov-er! Fate of friend, of wife, of lov-er, Trem-bles on a blow!

1. Loose the folds a-sunder, Flag we conquer un-der! The pla-cid sky now bright on high, Shall
2. Strands of life are riv-en; Blow for blow is giv-en, In dead-ly lock, or bat-tle shock, And

launch its bolts in thun-der! On-ward! 'tis our coun-try needs us!
"Mer-cy!" shrieks to heav-en! Men of Har-lech, young and hoa-ry,

He is brav-est, he who leads us! Hon-our's self now proud-ly heads us! Cambria, God, and Right!
Would you win a name in sto-ry? Strike for home, for life, for glo-ry! Cambria, God, and Right!

THE MAPLE LEAF FOR EVER.

The National Song of Canada.

Words and Music by Alexander Muir.

Con spirito.

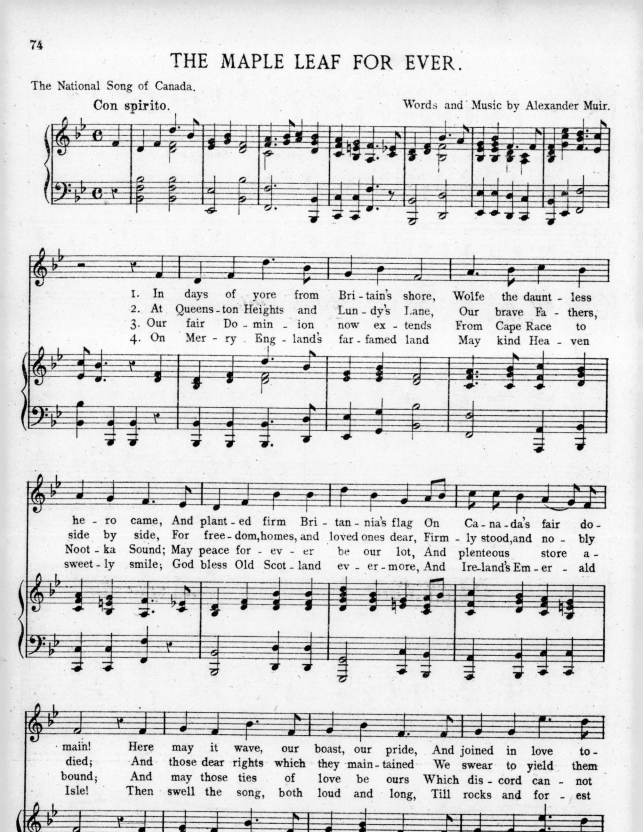

1. In days of yore from Britain's shore, Wolfe the dauntless he-ro came, And planted firm Britannia's flag On Canada's fair domain! Here may it wave, our boast, our pride, And joined in love to-
2. At Queenston Heights and Lundy's Lane, Our brave Fathers, side by side, For freedom, homes, and loved ones dear, Firmly stood, and nobly died; And those dear rights which they maintained We swear to yield them
3. Our fair Dominion now extends From Cape Race to Nootka Sound; May peace forever be our lot, And plenteous store abound; And may those ties of love be ours Which discord cannot
4. On Merry England's far-famed land May kind Heaven sweetly smile; God bless Old Scotland evermore, And Ireland's Emerald Isle! Then swell the song, both loud and long, Till rocks and forest

Included by kind permission of Messrs. A. & S. Nordheimer, Toronto, Canada.

1. ge-ther, The This-tle, Sham-rock, Rose en-twine The Ma-ple Leaf for - ev-er!
2. nev-er! Our watchword ev-er-more shall be, The Ma-ple Leaf for - ev-er!
3. sev-er; And flour-ish green o'er Freedom's home, The Ma-ple Leaf for - ev-er!
4. qui-ver, God save our King, and Hea-ven bless The Ma-ple Leaf for - ev-er!

1st Ten. CHORUS.

1. The Ma-ple Leaf, our em-blem dear, The Ma-ple Leaf for - ev-er! God
2. The Ma-ple Leaf, our em-blem dear, The Ma-ple Leaf for - ev-er! God

2nd Ten.

3. The Ma-ple Leaf, our em-blem dear, The Ma-ple Leaf for - ev-er! And
4. The Ma-ple Leaf, our em-blem dear, The Ma-ple Leaf for - ev-er! God

Bass.

save our King, and Hea-ven bless The Ma-ple Leaf for - ev-er!
save our King, and Hea-ven bless The Ma-ple Leaf for - ev-er!

flour-ish green o'er Free-dom's home, The Ma-ple Leaf for - ev-er!
save our King, and Hea-ven bless The Ma-ple Leaf for - ev-er!

THE STAR-SPANGLED BANNER.

National Song of the United States.

With spirit.

Arr. by J. K. L.

Oh! say can ye see, by the dawn's ear-ly light, What so proud-ly we hail'd at the

twi-light's last gleam-ing, Whose broad stripes and bright stars, thro' the per-il-ous fight, O'er the

ram-parts we watch'd, were so gal-lant-ly stream-ing, And the rock-ets' red glare, the shells

burst-ing in air, Gave proof thro' the night that our flag was still there.

Oh! say does that star-spangled ban-ner yet wave, O'er the land of the free, and the home of the brave?

CHORUS. tempo

Oh! say does that star-spangled ban-ner yet wave, O'er the land of the free, and the home of the brave?

2.

On the shore, dimly seen, through the mists of the deep,
    Where the foe's haughty host in dread silence reposes,
What is that which the breeze, o'er the towering steep,
    As it fitfully blows, half conceals, half discloses?
Now it catches the gleam of the morning's first beam,
In full glory reflected, now shines in the stream.
        'Tis the star-spangled banner! O long may it wave,
        O'er the land of the free, and the home of the brave!

3.

And where is that band who so vauntingly swore,
    'Mid the havoc of war, and the battle's confusion,
A home and a country they'd leave us no more?
    Their blood has washed out their foul footstep's pollution.
No refuge could save the hireling and slave,
From the terror of fight, or the gloom of the grave.
        And the star-spangled banner in triumph shall wave,
        O'er the land of the free, and the home of the brave!

4.

O, thus be it ever when freemen shall stand
    Between their loved home and the war's desolation;
Blest with vict'ry and peace, may the Heaven-rescued land
    Praise the Power that hath made and preserved us a nation.
Then conquer we must, for our cause it is just,
And this be our motto, "In God is our trust."
        And the star-spangled banner in triumph shall wave,
        While the land of the free is the home of the brave!

HAIL, COLUMBIA.

Words by Judge Hopkinson.(1798.)

Prof. Phylo.(1798.)
Arr. by W. H. M.

1. In - de - pen - dence be your boast; Be ev - er mind - ful
2. off' - ring peace sin - cere and just, In heav'n we place a
3. e - qual skill, with stea - dy pow'r, He go - verns in the
4. hope was sink - ing in dis - may, When gloom ob - scur'd Co -

what it cost: Be ev - er grate - ful for the prize, And
man - ly trust, That truth and jus - tice may pre - vail, And
fear - ful hour Of hor - rid war, or guides with ease The
lum - bia's day, His stea - dy mind, from chan - ges free, Re -

CHORUS.

let its al - tar reach the skies.
ev - 'ry scheme of bon - dage fail.
hap - pier time of hon - est peace.
solv'd on death or li - ber - ty.

Firm, u - ni - ted, let us be,

Rally - ing round our li - ber - ty, As a band of

bro - thers join'd, Peace and safe - ty we shall find.

JOHN BROWN'S BODY.

March-Song of the American War.

Alla marcia.

1. John Brown's body lies a mould'ring in the grave, John Brown's body lies a-
2. The stars of heaven are looking kindly down, The stars of heaven are

mould'ring in the grave, John Brown's body lies a-mould'ring in the grave, His soul is marching on!
looking kindly down, The stars of heaven are looking kindly down, On the grave of old John Brown.

CHORUS.

Glory! Glory Hallelujah! Glory! Glory Hallelujah!

Glory! Glory Hallelujah! His soul is marching on!

3. He's gone to be a soldier in the army of the Lord,
   His soul is marching on.
4. John Brown's knapsack is strapp'd upon his back,
   His soul is marching on.

5. His pet lambs will meet him on the way,
   And they'll go marching on.
6. We'll hang Jeff Davis on a sour apple tree,
   As we go marching on.

An effective way of singing this song is to repeat the first verse over and over, dropping a word from the end of the verse each time, until all the words are thus dropped; and filling out the time with silent beats, until the words "His soul is marching on" are reached. These, with the Chorus following, should be sung *forte* each time.

LA MARSEILLAISE.

Written and composed by
Claude Joseph Rouget de Lisle. (1792.)

Arr. for male voices by W. H. M.

Con anima.

1. Al - lons en - fants de la pa - tri - e, Le jour de
2. Que veut cet - te hor - de d'es - cla - ves, De traî - tres
3. Trem - blez, ty - rans et vous per - fi - des, L'op - pro - bre
1. Ye sons of France, a - wake to glo - ry! Hark, hark! what

gloire est ar - ri - vé. Con - tre nous de la ty - ran -
de rois con - ju - rés! Pour qui ces ig - no - bles en -
de tous les par - tis! Trem - blez, vos pro - jets par - ti -
my - riads bid you rise: Your chil - dren, wives, and grand - sires

ni - e, L'é - ten - dard sang - lant est le - vé, L'é - ten -
tra - ves, Ces fers, dès long - temps pré - pa - rés? Ces fers,
ci - des Vont en - fin re - ce - voir leur prix, Vont en -
hoa - ry: Be - hold their tears and hear their cries, Be - hold their

1. dard sang-lant est le - vé, En - ten - dez - vous dans les cam -
2. dès long-temps pré - pa - rés? Français! pour nous, ah! quel ou -
3. fin re - ce - voir leur prix. Tout est sol - dat pour vous com -
I. tears and hear their cries! Shall hate - ful ty - rants mis - chief

pag - nes Mu - gir ces fé - ro - ces sol - dats? Ils
tra - ge! Quels trans - ports il doit ex - ci - ter! C'est
bat - tre; S'ils tom - bent, nos jeu - nes hé - ros, La
breed - ing, With hire - ling hosts, a ruf - fian band, Af -

vien - nent, jus - que dans nos bras, E - gor - ger nos fils, nos com - pa - gnes!
nous qu'on o - se me - na - cer De rendre à l'an - tique es - cla - va - ge.
France en pro - duit de nou - veaux, Con - tre vous tous prêts à se bat - tre.
fright and de - so - late the land, While peace and li - ber - ty lie bleed - ing!

4.

Français! en guerriers magnanimes,
  Portez ou retenez vos coups;
Epargnez ces tristes victimes,
  A regret s'armant contre nous;
Mais le despote sanguinaire,
  Mais les complices de Bouillé_
Tous ces tigres qui sans pitié
Déchirent le sein de leur mère.
    Aux armes, etc.

5.

Amour sacré de la patrie,
  Conduis, soutiens nos bras vengeurs.
Liberté, Liberté chérie,
  Combats avec tes défenseurs:
Sous nos drapeaux que la victoire
  Accoure à tes mâles accents,
  Que tes ennemis expirants
Voient ton triomphe et notre gloire.
    Aux armes, etc.

2.

With luxury and pride surrounded,
  The vile, insatiate despots dare,
Their thirst of gold and power unbounded,
  To mete and vend the light and air.
Like beasts of burden would they load us —
  Like gods would bid their slaves adore —
  But man is man _ and who is more?
Then shall they longer lash and goad us?
    To arms, etc.

3.

Oh liberty! can man resign thee,
  Once having felt thy generous flame?
Can dungeons, bolts and bars confine thee,
  Or whips thy noble spirit tame?
Too long the world has wept, bewailing
  That falsehood's dagger tyrants wield —
  But Freedom is our sword and shield,
And all their arts are unavailing.
    To arms, etc.

DIE WACHT AM RHEIN.

Words by Max Schneckenburger, (1840.)
Translation by Edward Oxenford.

Carl Wilhelm, (1854.)
Arr. for male voices by W. H. M.

Con spirito.

SEMI-CHORUS.

1. *Es braust ein Ruf wie Don-ner-hall, Wie Schwert-ge-klirr und Wo-gen-prall: Zum*
2. *Durch Hun-dert-tau-send zuckt es schnell, Und al-ler Au-gen blit-zen hell: Der*
1. A voice is heard like thun-der loud, Like bil-lows' roar and ar-mour'd crowd; "The
2. A hun-dred thou-sand men are there, Who ev-er for the foe pre-pare; Like

Rhein, zum Rhein, zum deut-schen Rhein! Wer will des Stro-mes Hü-ter sein?
Deut-sche, bie-der, fromm und stark, Be-schirmt die heil-ge Lan-des-mark.
Rhine! The Rhine! The Ger-man Rhine! Who comes to guard these banks of mine?"
light-ning flash their watch-ful eyes, And he who moves the land-mark dies!

FULL CHORUS.

Lieb' Va-ter-land! magst ru-hig sein, Lieb' Va-ter-land! magst ruhig sein; Fest steht und treu die Wacht, die
Dear Fa-therland! All fears re-sign! Dear Fa-therland! all fears re-sign! True are the hearts who watch, who

cres.

| Wacht | am | Rhein! | Fest steht und | treu die Wacht, die | Wacht | am | Rhein! |
| watch | the | Rhine! | True are the | hearts who watch, who | watch | the | Rhine! |

3.

So lang ein Tropfen Blut noch glüht,
Noch eine Faust den Degen zieht,
Und noch ein Arm die Büchse spannt,
Betritt kein Feind hier deinen Strand.
    Lieb' Vaterland! etc.

4.

Der Schwur erschallt, die Woge rinnt,
Die Fahnen flattern hoch im Wind;
Am Rhein, am Rhein, am deutschen Rhein,
Wir alle wollen Hüter sein!
    Lieb' Vaterland! etc.

3.

So long as life-blood still shall flow,
Or sword be left to strike a blow,
Whilst arm be left the gun to bear,
No foeman's foot shall venture there!
    Dear Fatherland, etc.

4.

Our oath resounds! The stream flows by!
Our banners proudly wave on high!
The Rhine! The Rhine! The German Rhine!
Our lives till death are ever thine!
    Dear Fatherland, etc.

RUSSIAN NATIONAL ANTHEM.

Music by General Alexis Lwoff. (1830.)
Arr. for male voices by W. H. M.

Maestoso.

God	the all	ter-	ri-	ble,	Thou	who or-	dain-	est	Thun-	der Thy
God	the all	mer-	ci-	ful,	earth	hath for-	sa-	ken	Thy	ho- ly
God	the om-	ni-	po-	tent,	might- y	a-	ven-	ger,	Watch-	ing in-

cla-	rion and	light-	ning Thy	sword,	Show	forth Thy	pi-	ty	on
ways,	and hath	slight-	ed Thy	word;	Let	not thy	wrath	in	its
vi- si-	ble,	judg-	ing un-	heard,	Save	us in	mer-	cy,	and

high when Thou	reign- est,	Give	to	us	peace	in our	time,	O	Lord.
ter- ror a-	wa- ken,	Give	to	us	peace	in our	time,	O	Lord.
save	us in	dan- ger,	Give	to	us	peace	in our	time,	O	Lord.

AUSTRIAN NATIONAL ANTHEM.

Words by Baron Zedlitz.
Translation by Edward Oxenford.

Joseph Haydn. (1797.)
Arr. for male voices by W. H. M.

1.
Gott er-hal-te Franz den Kai-ser, un-sern gu-ten Kai-ser Franz!
Hoch als Herr-scher, hoch als Wei-ser, steht er in des Ruh-mes Glanz!

1.
God pre-serve our gra-cious Emp'-ror, Franz our sov'-reign, great is he!
Wise as Ru-ler, deep in knowledge, Na-tions his re-nown may see!

Lie-be win-det Lor-beer-rei-ser Ihm zum e-wig grü-nen Kranz!
Love en-twines a crown of lau-rel That shall all un-fad-ing be;

Gott er-hal-te Franz den Kai-ser, un-sern gu-ten Kai-ser Franz!
God pre-serve our gra-cious Emp'-ror, Franz our sov'-reign, great is he!

2.

Ueber blühende Gefilde
 Reicht sein Scepter weit und breit;
Säulen seines Throns sind Milde,
 Biedersinn und Redlichkeit,
Und von seinem Wappenschilde
 Strahlet die Gerechtigkeit.
  Gott erhalte, etc.

3.

Sich mit Tugenden zu schmücken,
 Achtet er der Sorgen wert:
Nicht um Völker zu erdrücken
 Flammt in seiner Hand das Schwert.
Sie zu segnen, zu beglücken,
 Ist der Preis, den er begehrt.
  Gott erhalte, etc.

4.

Er zerbrach der Knechtschaft Bande,
 Hob zur Freiheit uns empor!
Früh erleb' er deutscher Lande,
 Deutscher Völker höchsten Flor,
Und vernehme noch am Rande
 Später Gruft der Enkel Chor:
  Gott erhalte, etc.

2.

O'er a vast and mighty Empire
 Rules our Sov'reign day by day;
Though he wields a potent sceptre,
 All beneficent his sway!
From his shield the Sun of Justice
 Ever casts its purest ray!
  God preserve, etc.

3.

To adorn himself with virtues
 He, and all successful, tries;
Ne'er against his loving people
 Does his hand in anger rise!
No! to see them free and happy,
 This he holds the highest prize.
  God preserve, etc.

4.

Pioneer of perfect freedom,
 Blessings round his footsteps cling!
To its pinnacle of greatness
 Soon may he his country bring!
And when death at last approaches
 Shall his grateful people sing:
  God preserve, etc.

SÖNNER AF NORGE.

Den Norske Nationalsang.

Words by Henr. Ank. Bjerregaard.
Translation by W. A. Craigie.

Norse National Air, by C. Blom.

Allegro con spirito.

1. Sön - ner af Nor - ge, det æld-gam - le Ri - ge, Sjun - ger til Har - pens den
1. Chil - dren of Nor - way, the an - cient of na - tions, Sing to the harp with a

fest - li - ge Klang! Man - digt og höj - tids - fuldt To - nen lad Sti - ge,
joy - ous re-frain, Man - ful - ly, so - lemn - ly raise your o - va - tions,

Fæd - re - ne - lan - det ind - vies vor Sang. Fæd - re - ne - min - der
Sound for our coun - try a glo - ri - ous strain. Fame of our fa - thers

her - ligt op - rin - der, Hver - gang vi næv - ne vor Fæd - re - ne - stavn,
round us there ga - thers, Oft as our race and our land we pro - claim,

Svul - men - de Hjer - ter og glöd - en - de Kin - der Hyl - de det elsk - te, det hel - li - ge Navn.
Swel - ling of bo - soms and flush - ing of fa - ces Hon - our the dear - est and ho - li - est name.

2. Frihedens Tempel i Nordmandens Dale
   Stander saa herligt i Ly af hans Fjeld:
Frit tör han tænke, og frit tör han tale,
   Frit tör han virke til Norriges Held.
Fuglen i Skove, Nordhavets Vove,
   Friere er ei, end Norriges Mand:
Villig dog lyder han selvgivne Love.
   Trofast mod Konning og Fædreneland.

3. Elskede Land med de skyhöie Bjerge,
   Frugtbare Dale og fiskrige Kyst!
Troskab og Kjærlighed fro vi dig sværge;
   Kalder du, blöde vi for dig med Lyst,
Evig du stande, elskte blandt Lande,
   Frit som den Storm, der omsuser dit Fjeld!
Og, medens Bölgen omsnoer dine Strande,
   Stedse du voxe i Hæder og Held.

2. Freedom, her shrine with the Norseman uprearing,
   Dwells in the heart of his mountains at rest;
Free is his thought, and his speech is unfearing,
   Free will he work for his fatherland's best.
Birds in their motion, waves of the ocean,
   Children of Norway are freer than they:
Willingly yet to the Law their devotion,
   Homage to King and to Country they pay.

3. Dearest of lands with thy mountains of beauty,
   Fertile thy valleys and teeming thy shore!
Faith and devotion to thee is our duty,
   Gladly our life-blood for thee we will pour.
Stand thou unwearing, fame ever bearing,
   Free as the tempest that roars on the hill;
And while thy coast meets the billow unsparing,
   Fortune and Fame be thy heritage still.

THE SCOTTISH FATHERLAND.

Paraphrased from the "DEUTSCHES LIED" of Em. Geibel by John Addington Symonds.

Boldly.

Wilhelm Tschirch.

1. Know ye the land of birk and row - an, The
2. Know ye the folk so leal and come - ly, The
3. Know ye the heart re - nowned in sto - ry, The

land of strength and stur - dy pride? Know ye the land of brae and gow - an, Of
folk to truth and hon - our vowed? Who hide 'neath garb and ha - bit home - ly A
blood that nerved our fa - thers brave? Who fought on ev' - ry field of glo - ry For

pur - ple heath on far moor - side, The straths en - riched by heav'n's own dew, En - compass'd
heart as warm and free and proud As beat of yore beneath the plaid Of Bruce or
vic - t'ry or a he - ro's grave? Still glows the cour - age of our sires In us with

IN THE GARB OF OLD GAUL.

I.

In the garb of old Gaul, with the fire of old Rome,
From the heath-covered mountains of Scotia we come,
Where the Romans endeavoured our country to gain,
But our ancestors fought, and they fought not in vain.
 Such our love of liberty, our country, and our laws,
 That like our ancestors of old, we stand by freedom's cause;
 We'll bravely fight, like heroes bright, for honour and applause,
 And defy the French, with all their art, to alter our laws.

2.

No effeminate customs our sinews unbrace,
No luxurious tables enervate our race;
Our loud sounding pipe breathes the true martial strain,
And our hearts still the old Scottish valour retain. *Chorus.*

3.

As a storm in the ocean when Boreas blows,
So are we enraged when we rush on our foes;
We sons of the mountains, tremendous as rocks,
Dash the force of our foes with our thundering strokes. *Chorus.*

4.

We're tall as the oak on the mount of the vale,
Are swift as the roe which the hound doth assail;
As the full moon in autumn our shields do appear,
Minerva would dread to encounter our spear. *Chorus.*

5.

Quebec and Cape Breton, the pride of old France,
In their troops fondly boasted till we did advance;
But when our claymores they saw us produce,
Their courage did fail and they sued for a truce. *Chorus.*

6.

In our realm may the fury of faction long cease,
May our councils be wise, and our commerce increase;
And in Scotia's cold climate may each of us find
That our friends still prove true, and our beauties prove kind.
 Then we'll defend our liberty, our country, and our laws,
 And teach our late posterity to fight in freedom's cause;
 That they like our bold ancestors, for honour and applause,
 May defy the French, with all their art, to alter our laws.

IN THE GARB OF OLD GAUL.

Melody by General Reid.
(1720-1807.)

Boldly, in March Time.

In the garb of old Gaul, with the fire of old Rome, From the

heath-cov-er'd moun-tains of Sco - tia we come, Where the Ro-mans en-deav-our'd our

coun-try to gain, But our an - ces-tors fought and they fought not in vain.

FULL-CHORUS.

Such our love of lib - er - ty, our coun - try and our laws, That like our an - ces - tors of old, we stand by freedom's cause, We'll brave - ly fight, like heroes bright, for hon - our and ap - plause, And de - fy the French, with all their art, to al - ter our laws.

Soldier Songs and Sea Songs.

*"Lords of the wide world
and wild watery seas".*

Comedy of Errors, ii, 1.

FOR TO ADMIRE.

Words by Rudyard Kipling.

Music by Gerard F. Cobb.

3.
The things that was which I 'ave seen,
  In barrick, camp, an' action too,
I tells them over by myself,
  An' sometimes wonders if they're true;
For they was odd_ most awful odd_
  But all the same now they are o'er,
There must be 'eaps o' plenty such,
  An' if I wait I'll see some more.

4.
Oh! I 'ave come upon the books,
  An' frequent broke a barrick rule,
An' stood beside an' watched myself
  Be'avin' like a bloomin' fool.
I paid my price for findin' out,
  Nor never grutched the price I paid,
But sat in Clink without my boots,
  Admirin' 'ow the world was made.

5.
My girl she said, "Oh stay with me!"
  My mother 'eld me to 'er breast,
They've never written none, an' so
  They must 'ave gone with all the rest_
With all the rest which I 'ave seen
  An' found an' known an' met along.
I cannot say the things I feel,
  An' so I sing my evenin' song.

Words taken by Mr Kipling's kind permission from "The Seven Seas." (Methuen & Co.).

ship   is swep', the day   is done, The bu-gle's gone   for smoke an' play; An'
thinks   a-bout   the things   that was, An' leans an' looks a-cross the sea— Till,

black   a-gin' the   set-tin' sun The   Las-car sings *"Hum deck— ty hai!"*[1]
spite   of all   the   crowd-ed ship,There's no   one lef'   a - live   but me.

For   to ad-mire an'   for to   see,   For   to be-'old this world so wide— It

nev - er done no   good to me, But   I   can't drop it   if   I tried!

1. *i.e.* I'm looking out.

"BACK TO THE ARMY AGAIN."

Words by Rudyard Kipling.

Music by Gerard F. Cobb.

Allegro con spirito. Alla marcia.

1. I'm 'ere in a tick-y ul-ster an' a bro-ken bil-ly-cock 'at,_____ A lay-in' on to the ser-geant I
2. I done my six years' ser-vice, 'Er Ma-jes-ty sez: "Good-day,_____ You'll please to come when you're rung for, an'

3.

A man o' four-an'-twenty that 'asn't learned of a trade—
Beside "Reserve" agin' him— 'e'd better be never made.
I tried my luck for a quarter, an' that was enough for me,
An' I thought of 'Er Majesty's barricks, an' I thought I'd go an' see.

Words taken by M.ʳ Kipling's kind permission from "The Seven Seas." (Methuen & Cᵒ).

don't know a gun from a bat; ___ My shirt's do-in' du-ty for
'ere's your 'ole back-pay; ___ An' four-pence a day for

più lento

jack-et, my sock's stick-in' out o' my boots, An' I'm
bac-cy, an' bloom-in' gen-'r-ous too; An'

poco slentando

e espress.   *tempo primo*

learn-in' the damned old goose-step a-long o' the new re-
now you can make your for-tune the same as your orf'-cers

più lento e espress.   *tempo primo*

4.
The sergeant arst no questions, but 'e winked the other eye,
'E sez to me "Shun!" an' I shunted, the same as in days gone by;
For 'e saw the set o' my shoulders, an' I couldn't 'elp 'oldin' straight,
When me an' the other rookies come under the barrick gate.

5.
I took my bath, an' I wallered _ for, Gawd, I needed it so!
I smelt the smell o' the barricks, I 'eard the bugles go.
I 'eard the feet on the gravel _ the feet o' the men what drill _
An' I sez to my flutterin' 'eart-strings, I sez to 'em, "Peace, be still!"

f molto animato

cruits!
do?"} Back to the Ar-my a-gain, ser-geant,

f molto animato e sempre marcato

ad lib. e quasi parlante

Back to the Ar-my a-gain;_____ (Don't look so 'ard, for I

espress.   sf   sempre colla voce

a tempo

'ave-n't no card) I'm back to the Ar-my a-gain._____

espress.   rit.   a tempo

-- For this third line of the Refrain, in parenthesis, substitute

      (2) after the 2nd Verse:– ('Ow did I learn to do right-about turn?)

      (3)   „   „   3rd   „   ('Tisn't my fault if I dress when I 'alt_)

      (4)   „   „   4th   „   ('Oo would ha' thought I could carry an' port?)

      (5)   „   „   5th   „   (Out o' the cold an' the rain, sergeant.)

⊕--⊕ At the conclusion of the 5th Verse, substitute for this bar the first bar of next page, and go straight on.

TIM, THE DRAGOON.

Words by A. T. Quiller Couch. ("Q.")

Music by C. Villiers Stanford.

Words taken by kind permission from "Green Bays: Verses and Parodies," by Q. (Methuen & Co).

THE BRITISH GRENADIERS.

THE TARPAULIN JACKET.

Words by G. J. Whyte-Melville. (1821-78.)

Air by Charles Coote.

Moderato e tranquillo.

1. A tall stal-wart Lan-cer lay dy-ing, And as on his death-bed he lay, he lay, To his friends who a-round him were sigh-ing, These last dy-ing words he did say:—

CHORUS.

mf

Wrap me up in my tar-pau-lin jack-et,

mf

By permission of Messrs. Hopwood & Crew, 16 Mortimer Street, London, W.

jack - et, And say a poor buff - er lies low, lies low, And six stal - wart Lan - cers shall car - ry me, car - ry me, With steps so - lemn, mourn - ful, and slow.

2.

Had I the wings of a little dove,
    Far, far away would I fly, I'd fly,
Straight for the arms of my true love;
    And there would I lay me and die.
Chorus: Wrap me up, etc.

3.

Then get you two little white tombstones,
    Put them one at my head and my toe, my toe,
And get you a pen-knife and scratch there:
    "Here lies a poor buffer below."
Chorus: Wrap me up, etc.

4.

And get you six brandies and sodas,
    And set them all out in a row, a row,
And get you six jolly good fellows,
    To drink to this buffer below.
Chorus: Wrap me up, etc.

5.

And then in the calm of the twilight,
    When the soft winds are whispering low, so low,
And the darkening shadows are falling,
    Sometimes think of this buffer below.
Chorus: Wrap me up, etc.

THE YANG-TSI-KIANG.

Words by Thomas Davidson.

Music by Alison Hay Dunlop.

From Dr. James Brown's "Life of a Scottish Probationer," by permission of Messrs. Maclehose, Glasgow.

THE YANG-TSI-KIANG.

I.

My name is Polly Hill,
And I've got a lover Bill,
But he's caused me many a pang,
For his reg'ment got the rout,
And he's gone to the right about,
To the Yang-tsi-kiang.

2.

Oh! the war had broken out,
Though I don't know what about,
But they that make the wars go hang!
For he's gone with thousands ten
To fight the Chinamen
On the Yang-tsi-kiang.

3.

Oh! it's five years passed away,
Till it fell on a day,
As I sat by the door and sang,
That a soldier stopped and said,
"O, your lover Bill is dead
On the Yang-tsi-kiang.

4.

"It was in a tea-tree glen
That we met the Chinamen,
And one of the rogues let bang,
Which laid poor William low,
With his toe to the foe,
On the Yang-tsi-kiang.

5.

"'O, says poor Bill to me,
'Take this little sprig of tea,
And tell Poll where it sprang?
Now that was all he said,
When his head dropped like lead
On the Yang-tsi-kiang.

6.

"So here I hand to thee
This little sprig of tea,
'Twas by poor Bill's grave that it sprang;
You may keep it if you will,
As a souvenir of Bill
And the Yang-tsi-kiang."

7.

"Now, my soldier-boy," says I,
"Is there green in my eye?
(Pray, pardon me the use of slang,)
For I'm still your Polly Hill,
And you're welcome home, my Bill,
From the Yang-tsi-kiang."

THE LITTLE DRUMMER.

In marching time, and with spirit.

Music by Pohlenz.

1. Oh, I'm the lit-tle drum-mer lad,— And I make a dread-ful rat - tle! I'll lead you to pa-rade or bat - tle! Oh, I'm the boy to make you glad! When you drow-si - ly are sleeping, And the streets are hushed and still, Then I sound re-veil - lé, seem - ing To rouse both vale and

When this tattoo is over,
  And you hang upon my arm,
Treat me as your trusted lover,—
  Never let my heart beat alarm!

2.

Sweet! if only thou'lt be loving,
  Through whatever may befall,
Then truly thou'lt discover
  The meaning of my call!

Dirum, dirum! &c.

THE YOUNG RECRUIT.

Words by George Linley. (1798-1865.)

Music by Friedrich Kücken. (1855.)

In March Time.

1. See these rib - bons gai - ly stream - - ing, I'm a sol - dier now, Li - zette, I'm a sol - dier now, Li - zette, Yes, of bat - tle I am dream - - ing, And the hon - our I shall get.

2. We shall march a - way to - mor - - row, At the break - ing of the day, At the break - ing of the day, And the trum - pets will be sound - - ing, And the mer - ry cym - bals play;

3. Shame! Li - zette, to still be weep - - ing, While there's fame in store for me, While there's fame in store for me, Think when home I am re - turn - - ing, What a joy - ful day 'twill be,

Included by kind permission of Messrs. R. Cocks & Co., New Burlington Street, London.

111

SEMI-CHORUS.

With a sa - bre at my side, And a hel - met on my brow, And a
Yet be - fore I say good - bye, And a last sad part - ing take, As a
When to church you're fond - ly led, Like some la - dy smart - ly drest, And a

proud steed to ride, I will rush on the foe. Yes, I flat - ter me, Li -
proof of your love, Wear this gift for my sake; Then cheer up, my own Li -
he - ro you shall wed With a me-dal on his breast. Ha! there's not a maid - en

zette, 'Tis a life that well will suit The gay life of a young Re -
zette, Let not grief your beau - ty stain, Soon you'll see the Re - cruit a -
fair But with wel - come will sa - lute The gay bride of the young Re -

cres.

THE LEAD STRIKES ENGLISH GROUND.

Words by Joseph M. Emerson.

Music by Barry M. Gilholy.

1. The lead strikes Eng - lish ground, brave boys!
2. Through many a mid - night gale, brave boys!
3. Crowd on the wa - t'ry bul - wark - shrouds!

Rouse in the deep - sea line; We will not think of
We've prov'd our *O - cean Queen,* And shall we spare her
Each well-known cape and bay, We soon shall see their

Published separately in Keys B flat and C. Price 2/- Net.

8

peri - rils past Up - on the waste of brine. The
can - vas now, When the sea is rol - ling green? For
out - lines dim Rise o'er the bound - ing spray. And

main - yard fills, a - way, brave boys! Our chan - nel course is
many an an - xious eye is turn'd A - long the spark - ling
now, be - side the eve - ning hearth We come to take our

free; With flow - ing sheets she skims the waves That
foam: Crowd on, crowd on, they wait for us, To
place: On true hearts time can write no change, Though

fringe the sum - mer sea, That fringe the sum - mer sea.
breathe fond wel - come home, To breathe fond wel - come home.
wea - ther stain the face, Though wea - ther stain the face.

CHORUS.

Crowd on, brave boys, and give her cloth, From roy - al
truck to rail, She feels the chan - nel breeze, brave boys, And shall not want for sail.

HEART OF OAK.

Words by David Garrick. (1750.)

Music by Dr. Boyce.
Arr. for Male Voices with accomp. by J. K. L.

Boldly, in march time.

1. Come, cheer up, my lads, 'tis to glo-ry we steer, The prize more than all to an Eng-lish-man dear; To hon-our we call you, as free-men, not slaves,— For who are so free as the sons of the waves?

CHORUS.

Heart of oak are our ships! jol-ly tars are our men! We al-ways are read-y!

Stead-y, boys, stead-y! We'll fight and we'll con-quer a-gain and a-gain!

2.
We ne'er see our foes but we wish them to stay;
They never see us but they wish us away.
If they run, why, we follow, and run them ashore;
For if they won't fight us, we cannot do more.
  Heart of oak, etc.

3.
They swear they'll invade us, these terrible foes;
They frighten our women, our children, and beaus;
But, should their flat-bottoms in darkness get o'er,
Still Britons they'll find to receive them on shore.
  Heart of oak, etc.

4.
We'll still make them fear, and we'll still make them flee,
And drub 'em on shore, as we've drubb'd 'em at sea.
Then cheer up, my lads, with one heart let us sing,
Our soldiers, our sailors, our statesmen, our King.
  Heart of oak, etc.

5.
Still Britain shall triumph, her ships plough the sea,
Her standard be Justice, her watchword "Be free;"
Then cheer up, my lads, with one heart let us sing,
Our soldiers, our sailors, our statesmen, our King.
  Heart of oak, etc.

TOLL FOR THE BRAVE.

Words by William Cowper. (1782.)

Music by George Frederick Handel.
March from "Scipio" (1725.)

Toll for the Brave! The Brave that are no more, All sunk be-neath the wave, Fast by their na-tive shore! Eight hun-dred of the Brave, Whose cour-age well was tried, Had made the ves-sel heel, And laid her on her side; A land-breeze shook the shrouds, And she was o-ver-

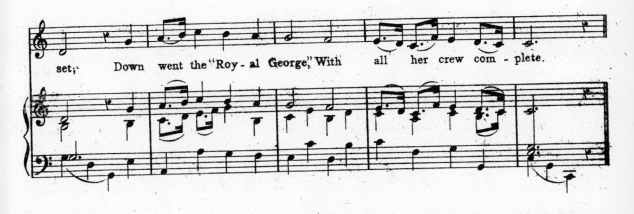

set; Down went the "Roy - al George," With all her crew com - plete.

CHORUS.

Toll for the Brave! The Brave that are no more, All

sunk be - neath the wave Fast by their na - tive shore!

2.

Toll for the Brave!
  Brave Kempenfelt is gone;
His last sea fight is fought;
  His work of glory done.
It was not in the battle,
  No tempest gave the shock,
She sprang no fatal leak,
  She ran upon no rock.
His sword was in its sheath,
  His fingers held the pen,
When Kempenfelt went down,
  With twice four hundred men. *Chorus.*

3.

Weigh the vessel up,
  Once dreaded by our foes,
And mingle with our cup
  The tears that England owes.
Her timbers yet are sound,
  And she may float again,
Full charg'd with England's thunder,
  And plough the distant main.
But Kempenfelt is gone,
  His victories are o'er,
And he and his eight hundred
  Must plough the wave no more! *Chorus.*

THE MERMAID.

Words by A. J. C.

Arr. by Michael Watson.

CHORUS.

Sing-ing, Rule Bri-tan-nia, Bri-tan-nia, rule the waves! And Bri-tons nev-er, nev-er, nev-er shall be mar-ri-ed to a mer-ma-id At the bot-tom of the deep blue sea.

2.

She raised herself on her beautiful tail,
And gave him her soft, wet hand,
"I've long been waiting for you, my dear,
Now welcome safe to land.
Go back to your messmates for the last time,
And tell them all from me,
That you're mar-ri-ed to a mer-ma-id
At the bottom of the deep blue sea."
Chorus. Singing, Rule, Britannia, etc.

3.

We sent a boat to look for him,
Expecting to find his corpse,
When up he came with a bang and a shout,
And a voice sepulchrally hoarse.
My comrades and my messmates,
Oh do not look for me,
For I'm mar-ri-ed to a mer-ma-id
At the bottom of the deep blue sea.
Chorus. Singing, Rule, Britannia, etc.

4.

In my chest you'll find my half-year's wage,
Likewise a lock of hair,
This locket from my neck you'll take,
And bear to my young wife dear.
My carte-de-visite to my grandmother take,
Tell her not to weep for me,
For I'm mar-ri-ed to a mer-ma-id
At the bottom of the deep blue sea.
Chorus. Singing, Rule, Britannia, etc.

5.

The anchor was weighed, and the sails unfurled,
And the ship was sailing free,
When up we went to our cap-i-taine,
And our tale we told to he.
The captain went to the old ship's side,
And out loud bellowed he,
"Be as happy as you can, with your wife, my man,
At the bottom of the deep blue sea."
Chorus. Singing, Rule, Britannia, etc.

THE MERMAID.

An old sea song.

Arr. by W. H. M.

Andante giocoso.

1. 'Twas Fri - day morn when we set sail, And we were not far from the land, When the
2. Then up spake the captain of our gallant ship, And a wellspoken man was he, "I have

Cap - tain he spied a love - ly mer - maid, With a comb and a glass in her
mar - ried me a wife in Sa - lem town, And to - night she a wid - ow will

hand, her hand, her hand, With a comb and a glass in her hand.
be, will be, will be, And to - night she a wid - ow will be."

CHORUS.

Oh! the o - cean wave may roll, And the storm - y winds may

blow, While we jol-ly sail-ors go skip-ping to the tops, And the

land-lub-bers ly-ing down be-low, be-low, be-low, And the land-lubbers ly-ing down be-low.

3.
Then up spake the cook of our gallant ship,
  And a fat old cook was he;
"I care much more for my kettles and my pots
  Than I do for the depths of the sea."— *Chorus.*

4.
Then out spake the boy of our gallant ship,
  And a well-spoken laddie was he;
"I've a father and mother in Boston city,
  But to-night they childless will be."— *Chorus.*

5.
"Oh, the moon shines bright and the stars give light,
  Oh, my mammy she'll be looking for me;
She may look, she may weep, she may look to the deep,
  She may look to the bottom of the sea."— *Chorus.*

6.
Then three times around went our gallant ship,
  And three times around went she,
Then three times around went our gallant ship,
  And she sank to the depths of the sea.— *Chorus.*

THE "GOLDEN VANITY."

Old English Ballad.

Traditional Air.
Arr. by John Tait.

With spirit. ♩ = 126.

A ship have I got in the North Coun-try, And she goes by the name of the "Gol-den Va-ni-ty;" O, I fear she'll be ta-ken by a Spa-nish Ga-la-lie,— As she sails by the Low-lands low, As she sails by the Low-lands low.

CHORUS.

By the Low-lands low, As she sails by the Low-lands low.

By the Low-lands low,

THE "GOLDEN VANITY."

1.

"A ship have I got in the North Country,
And she goes by the name of the "Golden Vanity;"
O, I fear she'll be taken by a Spanish Ga-la-lie,
    As she sails by the Low-lands low."

2.

To the Captain then upspake the little Cabin-boy,
He said, "What is my fee if the galley I destroy?
The Spanish Ga-la-lie, if no more it shall annoy,
    As you sail by the Low-lands low?"

3.

"Of silver and of gold I will give to you a store,
And my pretty little daughter that dwelleth on the shore,
Of treasure and of fee as well I'll give to thee galore,
    As we sail by the Low-lands low."

4.

Then the boy bared his breast, and straightway leaped in,
And he held in his hand an augur sharp and thin,
And he swam until he came to the Spanish galleon,
    As she lay by the Low-lands low

5.

He bored with the augur, he bored once and twice,
And some were playing cards, and some were playing dice;
When the water flowed in, it dazzled their eyes,
    And she sank by the Low-lands low.

6.*

So the Cabin-boy did swim all to the larboard-side,
Saying, "Captain! take me in, I am drifting with the tide!"
"I will shoot you! I will kill you!" the cruel Captain cried,
    "You may sink by the Low-lands low."

7.

Then the Cabin-boy did swim all to the starboard-side,
Saying, "Messmates, take me in, I am drifting with the tide!"
Then they laid him on the deck, and he closed his eyes and died,
    As they sailed by the Low-lands low.

8*

They sewed his body up, all in an old cow's hide,
And they cast the gallant Cabin-boy over the ship's side,
And left him without more ado a-drifting with the tide,
    And to sink by the Low-lands low.

* These two verses may be omitted in singing.

The Captain of the ballad is traditionally supposed to have been Sir Walter Raleigh, with the current estimate of whose character, it is said, the selfishness and heartless ingratitude of the Captain certainly agree.

TEN THOUSAND MILES AWAY.

Written and composed by J. B. Geoghegan.

Arr. by W. H. M.

Sing Ho! for a brave and a val-iant bark, And a brisk and live-ly breeze, A

joy-ial crew and a Cap-tain too, To car-ry me o-ver the seas, To

car-ry me o-ver the seas, my boys, To my true love so gay; She has

ta-ken a trip on a gal-lant ship Ten thou-sand miles a-way.

CHORUS.

So blow the winds, Heigh-ho; A-rov-ing I will go; I'll stay no more on
Heigh-ho! will go;

England's shore, So let the mu-sic play! I'll start by the morning train, To cross the rag-ing

main, For I'm on the move to my own true love, Ten thou-sand miles a-way.

2.

My true love, she is beautiful,
  My true love, she is young;
Her eyes are blue as the violet's hue,
  And silvery sounds her tongue—
And silvery sounds her tongue, my boys,
  But, while I sing this lay,
She is doing the grand in a distant land,
  Ten thousand miles away.

3.

Oh! that was a dark and dismal day
  When last she left the strand.
She bade good-bye, with a tearful eye,
  And waved her lily hand—
And waved her lily hand, my boys,
  As the big ship left the bay;
"Adieu," says she, "remember me,
  Ten thousand miles away."

4.

Oh! if I could be but a bo's'n bold,
  Or only a bombardier,
I'd hire a boat and hurry afloat,
  And straight to my true love steer—
And straight to my true love steer, my boys,
  Where the dancing dolphins play,
And the whales and the sharks are having their larks,
  Ten thousand miles away.

5.

Oh! the sun may shine through a London fog,
  And the Thames run bright and clear,
The ocean's brine be turned to wine,
  And I may forget my beer—
And I may forget my beer, my boys,
  And landlord's quarter-day;
But I'll never part from my own sweetheart,
  Ten thousand miles away!

A CAPITAL SHIP.

Words from *St. Nicholas*. Air—"Ten Thousand Miles away."

1.

A capital ship for an ocean trip
  Was the Walloping Window Blind!
No wind that blew dismayed the crew
  Or troubled the captain's mind;
The man at the wheel was made to feel
  Contempt for the wildest blow-ow-ow,
Though it often appeared, when the gale had cleared,
  That he'd been in his bunk below.
Chorus. Then blow, ye winds, heigh-ho!
      A-roving I will go!
    I'll stay no more on England's shore,
      So let the music play-ay-ay!
    I'm off for the morning-train!
      I'll cross the raging main!
    I'm off to my love with a boxing glove,
      Ten thousand miles away!

2.

The bo'swain's mate was very sedate,
  Yet fond of amusement too;
He played hop-scotch with the starboard watch,
  While the captain, he tickled the crew!
And the gunner we had was apparently mad,
  For he sat on the after-rai-ai-ail,
And fired salutes with the captain's boots
  In the teeth of the booming gale!
Chorus. Then blow, etc.

3.

The captain sat on the commodore's hat
  And dined, in a royal way,
Off toasted pigs and pickles and figs
  And gunnery bread each day.
And the cook was Dutch, and behaved as such;
  For the diet he gave the crew-ew-ew
Was a number of tons of hot-cross-buns
  Served up with sugar and glue.
Chorus. Then blow, etc.

4.

All nautical pride we laid aside,
  And we ran the vessel ashore
On the Gulliby Isles, where the Poopoo smiles;
  And the rubbly Ubdugs roar;
And we sat on the edge of a sandy ledge
  And shot at the whistling bee-ee-ee;
And the cinnamon bats wore waterproof hats
  As they dipped in the shiny sea.
Chorus. Then blow, etc.

5.

On Rugbug bark, from morn till dark,
  We dined till we all had grown
Uncommonly shrunk; when a Chinese junk
  Came up from the Torriby Zone.
She was chubby and square, but we didn't much care,
  So we cheerily put to sea-ea-ea;
And we left all the crew of the junk to chew
  On the bark of the Rugbug tree.
Chorus. Then blow, etc.

BEN BACKSTAY.

2.

Once sailing with a captain,
  Who was a jolly dog,
Our Ben and all his messmates got
  A double share of grog.
    Chorus.—With a chip, chop, etc.

3.

So Benny he got tipsy.
  Quite to his heart's content,
And leaning o'er the starboard side
  Right overboard he went.
    Chorus.—With a chip, chop, etc.

4.

A shark was on the starboard side,
  And sharks no man can stand,
For they do gobble up everything
  Just like the sharks on land.
    Chorus.—With a chip, chop, etc.

5.

They threw him out some tackling
  To give his life a hope;
But as the shark bit off his head
  He couldn't see the rope,
    Chorus.—With a chip, chop, etc.

6.

At twelve o'clock his ghost appeared
  Upon the quarter deck,
"Ho, pipe all hands ahoy!" it cried,
  "From me a warning take."
    Chorus.—With a chip, chop, etc.

7.

"Through drinking grog I lost my life,
  The same fate you may meet;
So never mix your grog too strong,
  But always take it *neat.*"
    Chorus.—With a chip, chop, etc.

A-ROVING.

Allegretto.

SOLO. ... *CHORUS.* ... *SOLO.*

1. At num-ber three Old Eng-land Square, (Mark well what I do say;) At num-ber three Old Eng-land Square, My Nan-cy Daw-son she lived there: And I'll go no more a-rov-ing With you, fair maid!

f CHORUS.

A-rov-ing! A-rov-ing! Since rov-ing's been my ru-i-in, I'll go no more a-rov-ing With you, fair maid!

2.
My Nancy Dawson she lived there,
Mark well what I do say;
She was a lass surpassing fair,
She'd bright blue eyes and golden hair;
And I'll go no more a-roving
With you, fair maid. *Chorus.*

3.
I met her first when home from sea,
Mark well what I do say;
Home from the coast of Africkee,
With pockets lined with good monie;
And I'll go no more a-roving
With you, fair maid. *Chorus.*

4.
Oh! didn't I tell her stories true,
Mark well what I do say;
And didn't I tell her whoppers too!
Of the gold we found in Timbuctoo;
And I'll go no more a-roving
With you, fair maid. *Chorus.*

5.
But when we'd spent my blooming "screw,"
Mark well what I do say;
And the whole of the gold from Timbuctoo,
She cut her stick and vanished too;
And I'll go no more a-roving
With you, fair maid. *Chorus.*

YE MARINERS OF ENGLAND.

Words by Thomas Campbell. (1777-1844.)

Allegro non troppo.

Music by H. Hugo Pierson.
(1816 - 73.)

Songs of Love.

"What signifies the life o' man
An 'twere na for the lasses, O!"

BURNS, Green grow the rashes.

GREEN GROW THE RASHES, O!

Words by Robert Burns, (1786.)

Air considerably before 1740.
Arr. by W. Augustus Barratt.

1. There's nought but care on ev-'ry han', In ev-'ry hour that pass-es, O; What
2. The warld-ly race may rich-es chase, An' rich-es still may fly them, O; An'
3. Gie me a can-ny hour at e'en, My arms a-bout my dea-rie, O; An'
4. For you sae douce, ye sneer at this, Ye're nought but senseless ass-es, O; The
5. Auld Na-ture swears, the love-ly dears Her no-blest work she class-es, O; Her

sig - ni-fies the life o' man, An' 'twere na for the lass-es, O!
tho' at last they catch them fast, Their hearts can ne'er en-joy them, O!
warld - ly cares, an' warld-ly men, May a' gae tap-sal-tee-rie, O!
wis - est man the warl' e'er saw, He dear-ly lo'ed the lass-es, O!
pren - tice han' she tried on man, An' then she made the lass-es, O!

Tenor. f

Green grow the rash - es, O! Green grow the rash - es, O! The

Basses to accentuate the melody.

sweet - est hours that e'er I spend Are spent a-mang the lass - es, O!

PER SECALE.

Words by John Smith, M. D., L L. D., etc.

Air, "Comin' thro' the Rye."
Arr. by John Tait.

LASSES OF SCOTLAND.

Words by J. W. Brodie-Innes, LL.B., Advocate.

Irish Melody.
Arr. by J. K. L.

1. You talk of your beau-ties of France and of Ger-ma-ny— Fris-ky and fro-lic-some, se-rious and ser-mo-ny; Still for the rar-est pro-duc-tion of har-mo-ny Las-ses of Scot-land are first on the call. Here's a health to the maids of the North, Round from the Clyde to the shores of the Forth, Coun-try and ci-ty girls, Clev-er and wit-ty girls, Dain-ty and pret-ty girls, Drink to them all.

CHORUS.

Here's a health to the maids of the North, Round from the Clyde to the shores of the Forth,

Country and ci-ty girls, Clev-er and wit-ty girls, Dain-ty and pret-ty girls, Drink to them all.

2.

Each is a queen in her own singularity,
Whether her tresses are raven or carroty,
Whether her features be dove-like or parroty,
   Whether her figure be dumpy or tall.
Drink! I'll give you the very best toast,
Each to the lass that he worships the most.
    Oh such variety
    In their society!
    Never satiety
     On us can fall. *Chorus.*

3.

Then every part they can fill with facility,
From scullery maid to the pink of nobility;
All that they tackle is done with ability—
   Not worth the doing is all they do not.
Drink, then, lustily, each to his lass!
Shout for the honours and empty the glass.
    Pay them your duties then,
    Worship their shoe-ties then,
    Rare Scottish beauties – they're
    Queens of the lot. *Chorus.*

4.

Sure every true lover may find his divinity;
Never roam far, then, but round your vicinity;
Seek till you find her, your choicest affinity—
   Never a fear that the maid will say nay.
Drink, then, draining a bumper with me,
Lasses of Scotland with thirty times three!
    Boys, do not tarry then,
    Sheer pluck will carry them;
    Woo them and marry them—
    Never delay! *Chorus.*

DRINK TO ME ONLY.

Words by Ben Jonson. (1574 - 1637.)

Old Melody.
Arr. by W. Augustus Barratt.

Andantino con grazioso.

1. Drink to me on - ly with thine eyes, And I will pledge with
2. I sent thee late a ro - sy wreath, Not so much hon' - ring

mine; Or leave a kiss with - in the cup, And I'll not look for
thee, As giv - ing it a hope that there It could not wi - ther'd

wine. The thirst that from the soul doth rise Doth ask a drink di - vine;
be; But thou there-on didst on - ly breathe, And sent'st it back to me;

But might I of Jove's nec - tar sip, I would not change for thine.
Since when it grows, and smells, I swear, Not of it - self, but thee.

PASSING BY.

Words by Robert Herrick (1591-1674.)

Music by Edward C. Purcell.

THE MANLY HEART.

Words by George Wither. (1588 - 1667.)

Music by G. Barker.

Andante con moto.

1. Shall I, wast - ing in des - pair, Die be - cause a wo - man's fair? Or make pale my cheeks with care, Be - cause an - o - ther's ro - sy are? Be she fair - er than the day,

Or the flow-'ry meads in May, If she think not well of me,

What care I how fair she be? What care I for whom she be?

last verse

2.

Shall my silly heart be pined
'Cause I see a woman kind;
Or a well disposéd nature
Joinéd with a lovely feature?
Be she meeker, kinder, than
Turtle-dove or pelican,
  If she be not so to me,
  What care I how kind she be?

3.

Shall a woman's virtues move
Me to perish for her love?
Or her well-deservings known,
Make me quite forget mine own?
Be she with that goodness blest
Which may merit name of Best,
  If she be not such to me,
  What care I how good she be?

4.

'Cause her fortune seems too high,
Shall I play the fool and die?
She that bears a noble mind
If not outward helps she find,
Thinks what with them he would do
Who without them dares her woo;
  And unless that mind I see,
  What care I how great she be?

5.

Great or good, or kind or fair,
I will ne'er the more despair;
If she love me, this believe,
I will die ere she shall grieve;
If she slight me when I woo,
I can scorn and let her go;
  For if she be not for me,
  What care I for whom she be?

TO ANTHEA.

Words by Robert Herrick (1591-1674).

Music by John L. Hatton (1809-1886).

Bid me to live, and I will live, Thy Pro-test-ant to be; Or bid me love, and I will give A lov-ing heart to thee, ___ A heart as soft, a heart as kind, A heart as sound and free, ___ As in the whole world thou canst find, That heart I'll give to

thee.

Bid that heart stay, and it will stay To hon-our thy de-

cres.

cree;_____ Or bid it lan-guish quite a-way, And't shall do so for

thee. Bid me to weep, and I will weep, While I have eyes to

see; And hav-ing none, yet I will keep A heart to weep for

SALLY IN OUR ALLEY.

H. Carey.
Arr. by W. H. M.

Allegretto.

Of all the girls that are so smart There's none like pret-ty Sal-ly, She is the
Of all the days that's in the week I dear-ly love but one day, And that's the
When Christmas comes a-bout a-gain O then I shall have money; I'll hoard it
My mas-ter and the neighbours all Make game of me and Sal-ly, And but for

dar-ling of my heart And lives in our al-ley; There is no la-dy in the
day that comes be-twixt A Sat-ur-day and Monday: For then I'm drest all in my
up with box and all And give it to my hon-ey: Would it were twice ten thousand
her I'd bet-ter be A slave and row a gal-ley; But when my seven long years are

land That's half so sweet as Sal-ly, She is the dar-ling of my heart, And
best, To walk a-broad with Sal-ly, She is the dar-ling of my heart, And
pounds, I'd give it all to Sal-ly, She is the dar-ling of my heart, And
out, I then will mar-ry Sal-ly, And hap-py ev-er strive to live, But

lives in our al-ley.
lives in our al-ley.
lives in our al-ley.
not in our al-ley.

AYE WAUKIN', O!

Arr. by W. Augustus Barratt

Adagio. *Somewhat sad.*

1. O I am wat, wat, O, I'm wat and wea - ry; Yet
2. Sim-mer's a plea-sant time, Flowers o' ev - 'ry col - our; The

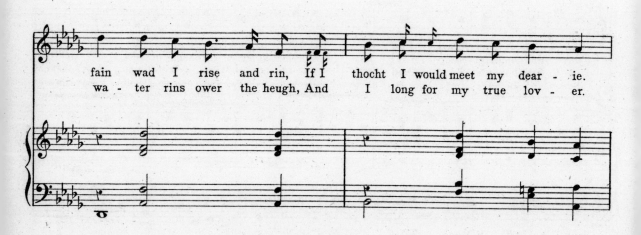

fain wad I rise and rin, If I thocht I would meet my dear - ie.
wa - ter rins ower the heugh, And I long for my true lov - er.

3.

When I sleep I dream,
When I wauk I'm eerie,
Sleep I can get nane
For thinkin' o' my dearie.

4.

Lanely nicht comes on,
A' the lave are sleepin',
I think on my true love,
And blear my een wi' greetin'.

MY FAITHFUL FOND ONE.

Mo rùn geal, dìleas.

Translation from the Gaelic* by Prof. Blackie.

Old Highland Melody.
Arr. by W. Augustus Barratt.

Rather slowly, and with tenderness.

SOLO.

1. If wings were mine now to skim the brine now, And like a sea - gull to float me free, To Is - lay's shore now they'd bear me o'er now, Where dwells the maid - en that is dear to me. My

1. *Is truagh nach robh mi's mo rog - ha cèi - le, Air mul - lach shlèibh - te nam beann - tan mòr, 'Sgun bhi ga'r n-éis - deachd ùch eòin na spèu - ra, 'Sgu'n tu - gainn fhéin di na ceu - dan pòg!* Mo

CHORUS.

2.

O were I yonder with her to wander
   Beneath the green hills beside the sea,
With birds in chorus that warble o'er us,
   And ruth of kisses so sweet to me! *Chorus.*

2.

Thug mi còrr agus naoi miosan,
   Anns na h-Innsean a b'fhaide thall;
'S bean bòidh' chead d'aodainn cha robh ri fhaotainn
   'S ged gheobhainn saoghal cha'n fhanainn ann. Chorus.

3.

What though the sky here be wet or dry here,
   With peaceful breeze here, or windy war;
In winter glooming or summer blooming,
   'Tis all one season, love, when thou art far! *Chorus.*

3.

Thug mi mios ann am fiabhrus claoidhte,
   Gun dùil rium oidhche gu'm bithinn beò;
B'e fàth mo smaointean a là's a dh-oidhche
   Gu'm faighinn faochadh 'us tu bhi'm chòir. Chorus.

THE BOATMAN.

(Fhir a Bhata.)

* Words translated from the Gaelic by
Thomas Pattison.

Old Highland Melody
Arr. by W. Augustus Barratt.

Andantino.

1. How of-ten haunt-ing the high-est hill-top, I scan the

o-cean thy sail to see! Wilt come to-night, love, wilt come to-

mor-row, Or ev-er come, love, to com-fort me? Fhir a

CHORUS (in unison)

bha-ta, no ho-ro ei-le, Fhir a bha-ta, no ho-ro

* Translation republished from "Gaelic Bards" by kind permission of Mr. Archibald Sinclair, Glasgow.
"Fhir a bhata" (pronounced, Eer a vata) means, "O Boatman". "No horo eile" is merely a call.

ei - le, Fhir a bha - ta no ho - ro ei - le, O fare thee

well, love, wher - e'er thou be.

2.

They call thee fickle, they call thee false one,
   And seek to change me; but all in vain.
No! thou'rt my dream yet, throughout the dark night,
   And ev'ry morn yet I watch the main. *Chorus.*

3.

There's not a hamlet, too well I know it,
   Where you go wand'ring or stay awhile,
But all its old folk you win with talking,
   And charm its maidens with song and smile. *Chorus.*

4.

Dost thou remember the promise made me,
   The tartan plaidie, the silken gown,
The ring of gold with thy hair and portrait?
   That gown and ring I will never own. *Chorus.*

HO-RO, MY NUT-BROWN MAIDEN.

(Ho-ro Mo nighean donn, bhòidheach.)

Translation from the Gaelic* by Professor Blackie.

Old Highland Melody.
Arr. by W. Augustus Barratt.

Moderate time and well marked.

Ho - ro, my nut-brown maid - en, Hi ri, my nut-brown maid - en, Ho - ro - ro, maid - en! Oh she's the maid for me.

Ho - ro, mo nighean donn, bhòidh - each, Hi ri, mo nighean donn, bhòidheach, Mo chaileag laghach bhòidh - each, Cha phòs - ainn ach thu.

SOLO.

1. Her eye so mild-ly beam - ing, Her look so frank and free, In

1. A Phei - gidhonn nam blàth - shul, Gur trom a thug mi gradh dhuit, Tha

CHORUS.

wak - ing and in dream - ing, Is ev - er - more with me. Ho - ro
d'iomhaighghaoil,'us dàill-eachd, A ghnàthtigh'nn fo m' uidh. Ho -

2.

O Mary, mild-eyed Mary,
  By land, or on the sea,
Though time and tide may vary,
  My heart beats true to thee.
    Ho - ro, etc.

3.

And since from thee I parted,
  A long and weary while,
I wander heavy-hearted
  With longing for thy smile.
    Ho - ro, etc.

4.

In Glasgow and Dunedin
  Were maidens fair to see,
But never a Lowland maiden
  Could lure mine eyes from thee;
    Ho - ro, etc.

5.

Mine eyes that never vary
  From pointing to the glen
Where blooms my Highland Mary
  Like wild-rose neath the Ben.
    Ho - ro, etc.

6.

And when with blossoms laden
  Bright summer comes again,
I'll fetch my nut-brown maiden
  Down from the bonnie glen.
    Ho - ro, etc.

2.

'N uair bha mi ann ad làthair,
Bu shona bha mo làithean _
A' sealbhachadh do mhànrain,
  'Us àille do ghnùis.
    Ho - ro, etc.

3.

Ach riamh o'n dh' fhàg mi d'fhianuis,
Gu bheil mi dubhach, cianail;
Mo chridhe trom ga phianadh
  Le iarguin do rùin.
    Ho - ro, etc.

4.

Ge lurach air a' chabhsair
Na mnathan òga Gallda,
A rìgh! gur beag mo gheall-s'
  Air bhi sealltainn 'n an gnùis.
    Ho - ro, etc.

5.

Ach 'n uair a thig an Samhradh,
Bheir mise sgrìob do'n ghleann ud,
'S gu'n tog mi leam do'n Ghalldachd,
  Gu h-annsail, am flùr.
    Ho - ro, etc.

THE BROKEN RING.

Das zerbrochene Ringlein.

Words by Joseph von Eichendorff. (1812.)
English Adaptation by Frederic W. Farrar.*

Melody by F. Glück. (1814.)
Arr. by W. Augustus Barratt.

Allegretto.

1. *In ei - nem küh - len Grun - de, Da*
1. Where loud the mill - wheel roar - eth A -

geht ein Müh - len - rad ———— *Mein' Lieb - ste ist ver -*
mid the flash - ing foam, ———— The maid my heart a -

pp

schwun - den; Die dort ge - woh - net hat; ———— *Mein'*
dor - eth, Had there her old - en home, ———— The

pp

Lieb - ste ist ver - schwun - den, Die dort ge - woh - net hat.
maid my heart a - dor - eth, Had there her old - en home.

* By kind permission of the Very Rev. Dean Farrar.

THE BROKEN RING.

Das zerbrochene Ringlein.

1.

In einem kühlen Grunde,
Da geht ein Mühlenrad;
Mein' Liebste ist verschwunden,
Die dort gewohnet hat.

2.

Sie hat mir Treu' versprochen,
Gab mir ein'n Ring dabei;
Sie hat die Treu' gebrochen,
Mein Ringlein sprang entzwei.

3.

Ich möcht' als Spielmann reisen
Weit in die Welt hinaus,
Und singen meine Weisen
Und geh'n von Haus zu Haus.

4.

Ich möcht' als Reiter fliegen
Wohl in die blut'ge Schlacht,
Um stille Feuer liegen
Im Feld bei dunkler Nacht.

5.

Hör' ich das Mühlrad gehen;
Ich weiss nicht, was ich will—
Ich möcht' am liebsten sterben
Da wär's auf einmal still!

1.

Where loud the mill-wheel roareth
  Amid the flashing foam,
The maid my heart adoreth
  Had there her olden home.

2.

She gave a true-love token,
  She breathed a plighted vow;
That ring she gave is broken,
  That troth is slighted now.

3.

I long where blood is streaming
  To clash in fiery fight,
And by the camp-fires gleaming
  To lay me down at night.

4.

I long to cleave the billow,
  My wronged heart to beguile,
The heaving wave my pillow,
  My port some lonely isle.

5.

But when the mill-wheel boometh
  No hope, no change can cheer;
Despair my soul consumeth,
  And death alone is dear.

6.

Death, of the friends I number
  The kindliest and best,
In thee the wronged ones slumber,
  In thee the weary rest.

LEBEWOHL.

(Farewell.)

Volkslied, known in 1690.
Translation by Edward Oxenford. (1892.)

Friedrich Silcher. (1827.)
Arr. for male voices by W. H. M.

2.

Wenn zwei gute Freunde sind,
Die einander kennen
Sonn' und Mond bewegen sich,
Ehe sie sich trennen.
Wie viel grösser ist der Schmerz,
Wenn ein treu verliebtes Herz
In die Fremde ziehet!

3.

Dort auf jener grünen Au'
Steht mein jung frisch Leben;
Soll ich denn mein Lebenlang
In der Fremde schweben?
Hab' ich dir was Leids gethan,
Bitt' dich, woll's vergessen,
Denn es geht zu Ende.

4.

Küsset dir ein Lüftelein
Wangen oder Hände;
Denke, dass es Seufzer sei'n,
Die ich zu dir sende.
Tausend schick' ich täglich aus,
Die da wehen um dein Haus,
Weil ich dein gedenke.

2.

When two hearts as one entwine,
 Both with friendship beating,
Sun and moon should cease to shine
 Ere the final meeting!
How much greater is the woe,
 When a loving heart must go
 O'er the pathless ocean!

3.

Yonder lies my childhood's home;
 Hard it is to sever!
Must I o'er the surging foam
 Stay away for ever?
If I ever did thee wrong
Do not now my pain prolong,
 But at once forgive me!

4.

Should thy face a zephyr kiss,
 O'er the ocean flying,
'T will, in truth, be surely this,
 I for thee am sighing!
Thousands I shall send to thee,
For, though parted, thou wilt be
 Ever unforgotten!

TREUE LIEBE.

Volkslied of the Thuringian Forest.
Translation by Edward Oxenford.

German Folk-Melody.

Moderato.

1. Ach! wie ist's möglich dann, Dass ich dich lassen kann? Hab' dich von
   I. Ah! it is hard to say, That we must part to-day! Thou hast my

Herzen lieb, Das glaube mir. Du hast die Seele mein
heart's deep love, Thou knowest well! My soul is wholly thine,

So ganz genommen ein, Dass ich kein' and're lieb', Als dich allein!
And both so intertwine, None other could I love But thine alone!

2.

Blau ist ein Blümelein,
Das heisst Vergissnichtmein;
Dies Blümlein leg' an's Herz,
   Und denke mein!
Stirbt Blum' und Hoffnung gleich,
Wir sind an Liebe reich,
Denn die stirbt nie bei mir,
   Das glaube mir!

2.

Blue is a floweret
Called the forget-me-not;
Lay it on thy dear heart,
   Thinking of me!
If hope and flow'r should die,
Such is our constancy
Still would my love remain
   Faithful to thee.

3.

Wär'ich ein Vögelein,
Bald wollt' ich bei dir sein,
Scheut' Falk' und Habicht nicht,
   Flög' schnell zu dir.
Schöss' mich ein Jäger tot,
Fiel' ich in deinen Schoss;
Säh'st du mich traurig an,
   Gern stürb' ich dann.

3.

Would that a bird I were!
Soon would I speed through air,
Heeding not bird of prey,
   Flying to thee.
If a shaft wounded me,
Close would I fall to thee;
Then, if one tear thou shed,
   Gladly would die!

α.

Πῶς ποτ' ἐνέσσεταί
μοι σὲ μεθιέναι;
κάρτα φιλῶ σέ τοι
πείθεό μοι.
ἦτορ ἐμόν, πέπον,
σοῦ τελέως πλέον
οὔτιν' ἔχει φίλην
ἢ σὲ μόνην.

β.

Ἄνθος ἔφυ τέρεν
μνῆμα λέγουσ' ἔμεν·
τοῦτο πρόπηξον εὖ,
μνῆμ' ἄρ' ἐμεῦ·
ἔφθισεν ἔστιν ἃ
ἄνθος ἰδ' ἐλπίδα·
οὐκ ἂν ἔρως φθίνοι·
πείθεο μοι.

γ.

Ὄρνεον εἰ νυ ἦν,
ἦ τάχ' ἂν ἐπτάμην
ἅρπαγας οὐ τρέσας
σεῖο πέλας.
εἰ δέ μ' ἀγρεὺς βάλεν,
ἐς γόνυ σοὶ πεσών,
εἰ ῥ' ἔλεον βλέπες,
θνῆσκον ἑκών.

F. van Hoffs

THE LANDLADY'S DAUGHTER.
(Der Wirtin Töchterlein.)

Words by Ludwig Uhland. (1813.)
Translation by Edward Oxenford.

Folk-Melody of the 18th Century.

1. Es zo-gen drei Burschen wohl ü-ber den Rhein, Bei ei-ner Frau Wir-tin da kehr-ten sie ein, Bei ei-ner Frau Wir-tin da kehr-ten sie ein. "Frau Wir-tin, hat sie gut Bier und Wein? Wo hat sie ihr schö-nes Töch-ter-lein? Wo hat sie ihr schö-nes Töch-ter-lein?"

1. There once were three stu-dents who came o'er the Rhine, And en-ter'd an inn for a flag-on of wine, And en-ter'd an inn for a flag-on of wine. "O land-la-dy, keep you good vin-ta-ges, pray? And where is your pret-ty young daugh-ter to-day? And where is your pret-ty young daugh-ter to-day?"

2.

"Mein Bier und Wein ist frisch und klar,
Mein Töchterlein liegt auf der Totenbahr."
Und als sie traten zur Kammer hinein,
Da lag sie in einem schwarzen Schrein.

3.

Der erste, der schlug den Schleier zurück,
Und schaute sie an mit traurigem Blick:
"Ach, lebtest du noch, du schöne Maid!
Ich würde dich lieben von dieser Zeit!"

4.

Der zweite deckte den Schleier zu,
Und kehrte sich ab und weinte dazu:
"Ach, dass du liegst auf der Totenbahr!
Ich hab' dich geliebet so manches Jahr!"

5.

Der dritte hub ihn wieder sogleich
Und küsste sie auf den Mund so bleich:
"Dich lieb' ich immer, dich lieb' ich noch heut',
Und werde dich lieben in Ewigkeit."

2.

"My vintages all are as good as can be;
My daughter is lost now for ever to me!"
The students craved leave to behold the fair dead,
And stood in her presence, whose spirit had fled.

3.

The first raised the veil that was drawn o'er her face,
And gazed on the form wrapt in Death's cold embrace.
"Ah me! if on earth thou wert fated to stay,
Fair maid, I would love thee henceforth from to-day!"

4.

The next o'er her face drew the veil once again,
And murmured these words in a sorrowful strain:
"Oh! take from my heart this sad tribute of tears!
Fair maid, I have loved thee most fondly for years!"

5.

The third, thereupon, drew the veil from her brow,
And, kissing her, cried, "Oh, how beautiful thou!
I loved thee, yea, always; I love thee to-day;
And still shall I love thee for ever and aye!"

JUANITA.

Words by the Hon. Mrs. Norton.

Spanish Ballad.

1. Soft o'er the foun-tain, Ling-'ring falls the south-ern moon:
2. When in thy dream-ing, Moons like these shall shine a-gain,

Far o'er the moun-tain, Breaks the day too soon! In thy dark eyes'
And day-light beam-ing Prove thy dreams are vain, Wilt thou not, re-

splendour, Where the warm light loves to dwell, Wea-ry looks, yet ten-der,
lent-ing, For thine ab-sent lov-er sigh, In thy heart con-sent-ing

Speak their fond fare-well! Ni-ta! Ni-ta! Ask thy soul if
To a prayer gone by? Ni-ta! Ni-ta! Let me ling-er

Ni-ta! Jua-ni-ta!

we should part! Ni-ta! Ni-ta! Lean thou on my heart.
by thy side! Ni-ta! Ni-ta! Be my own fair bride.

Ni-ta! Jua-ni-ta!

Included by permission of Messrs. Chappell & Co, London.

MY BONNIE.

Andante.

dolce

1. My Bon - nie is o - ver the o - cean, My Bon - nie is o - ver the sea,
2. Oh, blow, ye winds, o - ver the o - cean, Oh, blow, ye winds, o - ver the sea,

My Bon - nie is o - ver the o - cean, Oh, bring back my Bon - nie to me.
Oh, blow, ye winds, o - ver the o - cean, And bring back my Bon - nie to me.

CHORUS. *p* *cres.*

Bring back, bring back, bring back my Bon - nie to me, to me.

Bring back, bring back, bring back my Bon - nie to me, to me.

p *f*

Bring back, bring back, Oh, bring back my Bon - nie to me.

Bring back, bring back, Oh, bring back my Bon - nie to me.

3.
Last night as I lay on my pillow,
Last night as I lay on my bed,
Last night as I lay on my pillow,
I dreamed that my Bonnie was dead. *Chorus.*

4.
The winds have blown over the ocean,
The winds have blown over the sea,
The winds have blown over the ocean,
And brought back my Bonnie to me. *Chorus.*

SONGS OF REVELRY.

"Drink, puppy, drink."

MIHI EST PROPOSITUM.

Words ascribed to Walter Map.
Translation by Leigh Hunt.

Music by R. L. de Pearsall.

Con moto.

The words of this Song are attributed to Walter de Map (less correctly, Mapes), born about 1137, a friend of Becket, in 1196 appointed Archdeacon of Oxford; author of many Latin satirical poems.
Music by permission of Messrs. Novello, Ewer, & Co., 1 Berners Street, London, W.

3.

Suum cuique proprium dat natura munus,
Ego nunquam potui scribere jejunus,
Me jejunum vincere posset puer unus,
Sitim et jejunium, odi tanquam funus.

4.

Tales versus facio, quale vinum bibo,
Neque possum scribere nisi sumpto cibo,
Nihil valet penitus, quod jejunus scribo;
Nasonem post calices carmine præibo.

5.

Mihi nunquam spiritus prophetiæ datur,
Non nisi cum fuerit venter bene satur,
Cum in arce cerebri Bacchus dominatur,
In me Phœbus irruit, ac miranda fatur.

3.

Every one by nature hath—a mould which he was cast in;
I happen to be one of those—who never could write fasting;
By a single little boy—I should be surpass'd in
Writing: so I'd just as lief—be buried, tomb'd and grass'd in.

4.

Just as liquor floweth good—floweth forth my lay so;
But I must moreover eat—or I could not say so;
Nought it availeth inwardly—should I write all day so;
But with God's grace after meat—I beat Ovidius Naso.

5.

Neither is there given to me—prophetic animation,
Unless when I have eat and drank—yea, ev'n to saturation;
Then in my upper storey-hath Bacchus domination,
And Phœbus rusheth into me, and beggareth all relation.

THE GOOD RHEIN WINE.

Words by James Reed.

Music by John Gray.

1. Pour out the Rhein wine! let it flow Like a free and bound-ing riv-er; Till
2. Pour out the Rhein wine ev - er-more! Let the gob-let ne'er be tir-ing; The
3. Pour out the Rhein wine! when each hand Doth grasp a brim-ming measure, The

sad - ness sinks and ev - 'ry woe Lies drown'd be - neath its waves for ev - er.
Po - et's song and the Sa - ge's lore And the Pa - triot's lof - ty soul in - spir-ing.
pledge shall be "Our Fa - ther - land," And Free - dom, Friendship, Love and Pleasure.

CHORUS.

For naught can cheer the hearts that pine, Like a deep, deep draught of the
For an off - 'ring meet at Free - dom's shrine, Is a deep, deep draught of the
Then Hurrah! for the land of the pur - ple vine, And a deep, deep draught of the

1. good Rheinwine, Like a deep,   deep draught,   Like a deep, deep draught of the
2. good Rheinwine, Is a deep,   deep draught,   Is a deep, deep draught of the
3. good Rheinwine, And a deep,   deep draught,   And a deep, deep draught of the

good,   Rhein wine, Like a   deep,   deep draught,   Like a a
good,   Rhein wine, Is a   deep,   deep draught,   Is a a
good,   Rhein wine, And a   deep,   deep draught,   And a a

deep, deep draught of the good Rheinwine.
deep, deep draught of the good Rheinwine.
deep, deep draught of the good Rheinwine.

EDITE, BIBITE.

German Words from Kindleben's Studentenliedern, (1781.)

Melody from Methfessel's Commers- und Liederbuch, (1818.)

Presto

1. *Ça ça ge - schmau - set, Lasst uns nicht rap - pel - köpf - isch sein!*
1. Loud let the glass - es clink, Drink deep, nor spare the flow-ing bowl!

Wer nicht mit hau - set, Der bleib' da - heim!
The man who fears to drink, Has no true soul.

E - di - te, bi - bi - te, col - le - gi - a - les, Post mul - ta sœ - cu - la, po - cu - la nul - la.

2.

Der Herr Professor
Liest heut' kein Collegium;
Drum ist es besser,
Man trinkt eins 'rum. Chorus.

3.

Auf, auf, ihr Brüder!
Erhebt den Bacchus auf den Thron,
Und setzt euch nieder,
Wir trinken schon. Chorus.

4.

Denkt oft, ihr Brüder,
An unsre Jugendfröhlichkeit,
Sie kehrt nicht wieder
Die gold'ne Zeit! Chorus.

2.

This is the student's hour,
The stern professor's work is done;
We own no other pow'r
Save wine and song. *Chorus.*

3.

Here rules the rosy god;
Exalt old Bacchus to his throne,
And, drawing round the bowl,
Serve him alone. *Chorus.*

4.

Enjoy, while powers remain,
Life's pleasures in their prime;
Old age brings not again
Youth's golden time. *Chorus.*

GOLDTHRED'S SONG.

Words from Sir Walter Scott's "Kenilworth".

Music by W. Augustus Barratt.

This song is published separately by Messrs. Boosey & Co., London.

A SONG OF WATER.

Adapted from the Platt-Deutsch
by Lord Neaves.

Music by Dr. T. W. Drinkwater.

I'm ve-ry fond of wa-ter And I drink it noon and night; Not Rechab's son or daugh-ter Had there-in more de-light.

1. I break-fast on it dai-ly, And nec-tar it doth seem, When once I've mix'd it gai-ly With su-gar and with cream. But I for-got to mention, That in it first I see, In-fused or in sus-pen-sion, Good Moch-a or Bo-hea, In-

CHORUS.

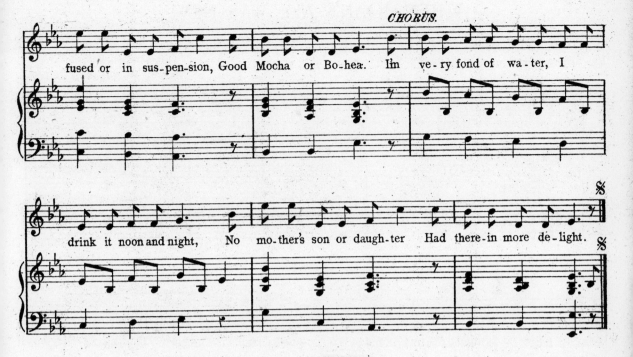

fused or in sus-pen-sion, Good Mocha or Bo-hea. Im ve-ry fond of wa-ter, I

drink it noon and night, No mo-ther's son or daugh-ter Had there-in more de-light.

2.

At luncheon, too, I drink it,
    And strength it seems to bring;
When really good, I think it
    A liquor for a King.
But I forgot to mention,—
    'Tis best to be sincere,—
I use an old invention
    That makes it into Beer. *Chorus.*

3.

I drink it, too, at dinner,
    I quaff it full and free,
And find, as I'm a sinner,
    It does not disagree.
But I forgot to mention,
    As thus I drink and dine,
To obviate distension
    I join some Sherry Wine. *Chorus.*

4.

And then, when dinner's over,
    And business far away,
I feel myself in clover,
    And sip my *eau sucrée.*
But I forgot to mention,
    To give the glass a smack,
I add, with due attention,
    Glenlivet or Cognac. *Chorus.*

5.

At last, when evening closes,
    With something nice to eat,
The best of sleeping doses
    In water still I meet.
But I forgot to mention,
    I think it not a sin,
To cheer the day's declension
    By pouring in some gin:
Chorus.   I'm very fond of water,
    It ever must delight
Each mother's son or daughter,
    When qualified aright.

WHEN JOAN'S ALE WAS NEW.

Old English Ballad
Re-written to suit modern times.*

Old English Ballad Air.
Arr. by W. Augustus Barratt.

Jovially.

There were three jo-vial fel-lows With lungs as black-smiths bel-lows, Sat drink-ing un-til mel-low, Be-lieve me, this was true. For each a pol-i-tic-ian stout Would arg-y-fy with

*) By kind permission of the Rev. S. Baring Gould, from his "Garland of Country Song" (London: Methuen & Co. 1895.)

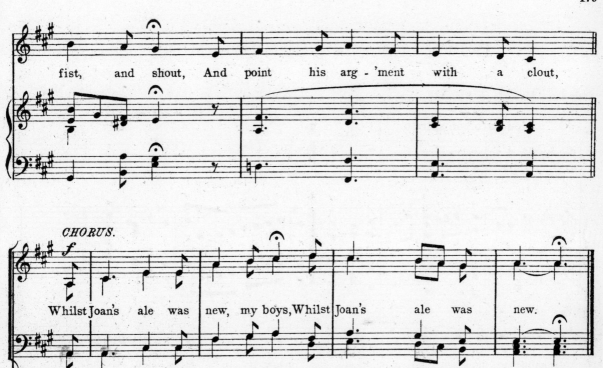

fist, and shout, And point his arg-'ment with a clout,

CHORUS.

Whilst Joan's ale was new, my boys, Whilst Joan's ale was new.

2.

The first he was a mason,
He swore that none could face'n
In point of edication,
   Amongst that jovial crew.
He pitched his hammer against the wall,
He hoped the church and tower would fall,
Then there'd be work for masons all, *Chorus.*

3.

The second he was a dyer,
He sat himself by the fire,
As proud as any squire,
   Amongst that jovial crew.
The House of Lords he would disgrace,
The Crown should have the bottom place,
The top, the dirtiest hands and face, *Chorus.*

4.

The third he was a tinker,
O'er one eye wore a blinker,
From ale he was no shrinker,
   Amongst that jovial crew.
The land, he said, should commons be,
To geese and men and asses free,
Then all would have equality, *Chorus.*

5.

The ale got in each head, sir,
Then each waxed wroth and red, sir,
And each to other said, sir,
   Believe me, this is true,
"The corner seat I'll have, for sure,"
For it they fought, they kicked, they swore,
Till all three sprawled upon the floor, *Chorus.*

DOWN AMONG THE DEAD MEN.

Words by John Dyer (1700-58.)

Old English Melody.
Arr. by W. H. M.

1. Here's a
2. Let

health to the king and a last - ing peace, To fac - tion an end, to
charm - ing beau - ty's health go round, In whom ce - les - tial

wealth in - crease! Come, let's drink it while we have breath, For
joys are found, And may con - fu - sion still pur - sue The

there's no drink - ing af - ter death. And he that will this health de - ny,
sense - less wo - man - hat - ing crew; And they that wo-man's health de - ny,

CHORUS.

Down a-mong the dead men, Down a-mong the dead men, Down, down,

down, down, Down a-mong the dead men let him lie!

3.

In smiling Bacchus' joys I'll roll,
Deny no pleasure to my soul;
Let Bacchus' health round briskly move,
For Bacchus is a friend to Love.
And he that will this health deny,
Down among the dead men let him lie!

4.

May love and wine their rites maintain,
And their united pleasures reign;
While Bacchus' treasure crowns the board,
We'll sing the joys that both afford.
And they that won't with us comply,
Down among the dead men let them lie!

HERE'S A HEALTH UNTO HIS MAJESTY.

Old English Toast.

Air by J. Savile.(1670.)
Arr. by W. Augustus Barratt.

Here's a health un- to His Ma-jes-ty, With a fa la la la la la la; Con-fu-sion to his en- e-mies, With a fa la la la la la la; And he that will not drink his health, I wish him nei- ther wit nor wealth, Nor yet a rope to hang him-self, With a fa la la la la la la la la la, With a fa la la la la la la.

HERE'S TO THE MAIDEN.

Words by Richard Brinsley Sheridan. (1776.)

Arr. by John Tait.

Allegro moderato.

1. Here's to the maid - en of bash-ful fif-teen, Now to the wi - dow of fif - ty;
2. Here's to the char - mer whose dimples we prize, Now to the dam - sel with none, sir;
3. Here's to the maid with a bo - som of snow, Now to her that's as brown as a ber - ry;
4. For let her be clum - sy or let her be slim, Young or an - cient, I care not a fea - ther, So

Here's to the flaunt-ing ex - tra - va-gant quean, And here's to the house-wife that's thrif - ty.
Here's to the girl with a pair of blue eyes, And now to the nymph with but one, sir.
Here's to the wife with a face full of woe, And here's to the dam - sel that's mer - ry.
fill up a bum-per, nay, fill to the brim, And e'en let us toast 'em to - ge - ther.

Let the toast pass, drink to the lass; I war - rant she'll prove an ex - cuse for the glass.
Let the toast pass, drink to the lass; I war - rant she'll prove an ex - cuse for the glass.
Let the toast pass, drink to the lass; I war - rant she'll prove an ex - cuse for the glass.
Let the toast pass, drink to the lass; I war - rant she'll prove an ex - cuse for the glass.

CHORUS.

Let the toast pass, drink to the lass; I war - rant she'll prove an ex - cuse for the glass.
Let the toast pass, drink to the lass, she'll prove an ex - cuse for the glass.

IN CELLAR COOL.

Rheinweinzecher.

German words by K. Müchler. (1802.)
Translation by Edward Oxenford. (1891.)

Melody by Ludwig Fischer. (1802.)
Arr. by W. H. M.

Moderato.

1. Im
1. In

küh - len Kel - ler sitz' ich hier, Auf ei - nem Fass voll Re - ben, Bin
cel - lar cool at ease I sit, Up - on a bar - rel rest - ing; In

fro - hen Muts und las - se mir vom al - ler - bes - ten ge - ben. Der
mer - ry mood I loud - ly call, The fin - est wine re - quest - ing. The

Kü - per zieht den He - ber voll, Ge - hor - sam mei - nem Win - ke, Reicht
cel - lar - man the beak - er fills, My lips I soon am link - ing, And

rall.

colla voce

mir das Glas, ich halt's em - por Und trin - ke, trin - ke, trin - ke.
deep and long the lus - cious draught I'm drink - ing, drink - ing, drink - ing!

2.

Mich plagt ein Dämon, Durst genannt,
  Doch um ihn zu verscheuchen,
Nehm' ich mein Deckelglas zur Hand
  Und lass' mir Rheinwein reichen.
Die ganze Welt erscheint mir nun
  In rosenroter Schminke;
Ich könnte niemand Leides thun,
  Ich trinke, trinke, trinke.

3.

Allein mein Durst vermehrt sich nur
  Bei jedem vollen Becner;
Das ist die leidige Natur
  Der echten Rheinwetnzecher!
Doch tröst' ich mich, wenn ich zuletzt
  Vom Fass zu Boden sinke:
Ich habe keine Pflicht verletzt,
  Denn ich trinke, trinke, trinke.

2.

That demon thirst is quite a plague,
  But, so that I may scare him,
Again I raise the beaker high,
  And, boldly quaffing, dare him.
The world seems cloth'd in rosy tints,
  Its clouds to tought are shrinking;
I feel a friend to ev'ry man
  While drinking, drinking, drinking!

3.

But still I find, the more I drink,
  The more my thirst increases;
In fact, a toper's lot is this—
  His craving seldom ceases!
Yet never mind, the day is long,
  And, till the sun is sinking,
My duty to good wine I'll do
  By drinking, drinking, drinking!

GRINDING.

Words by H. M. B. Reid. Air—"In Cellar Cool."

I.

In class-room cold I sit and con, from time of early matin,
With many a sigh and long-drawn yawn, my musty Greek and Latin.
I've store of flimsy German texts, in ugly yellow binding;
And all the gloomy morning through, I'm grinding, grinding, grinding.

2.

Long-winded Xenophon I cram, ἐνταῦθα's and ἐντεῦθεν's,
And Virgil's "pius" old grandam, with all his high-falutins;
The mists of Ciceronian phrase my aching eyes are blinding;
My nose is very cold, and still, I'm grinding, grinding, grinding.

3.

With "Ars Poetica" I'm vexed—Hexameters Homeric:
Euripides torments me next with tragedy hysteric:
The threads of Livy's prosy tale I'm painfully unwinding;
And still the hours drag slowly on— I'm grinding, grinding, grinding.

4.

I cannot take to Latin prose or Roman Literature,
The verbs in μι are deadly foes, — τύπτω I can't endure.
Unless from out this misery some way I'm quick in finding,
I'll sell my cribs, and bid farewell to grinding, grinding, grinding.

COME, LANDLORD, FILL THE FLOWING BOWL.

Arr. by J. K. L.

CHORUS.

Wake for the fal - al-al-al - i - do, Wake for the fal - al - al al - i - do, Wake for the fal - al - al - al - ay! To-mor - row is a ho - li - day.

2.

The man who drinketh small beer,
  And goes to bed quite sober,
Fades as the leaves do fade,
  That drop off in October. *Chorus.*

3.

The man who drinketh strong beer,
  And goes to bed right mellow,
Lives as he ought to live,
  And dies a jolly good fellow. *Chorus.*

4.

But he who drinks just what he likes,
  And getteth half-seas over,
Will live until he die perhaps,
  And then lie down in clover. *Chorus.*

5.

The man who kisses a pretty girl,
  And goes and tells his mother,
Ought to have his lips cut off,
  And never kiss another. *Chorus.*

VIVE L'AMOUR.

Allegro molto.

Accomp. by J. K. L.

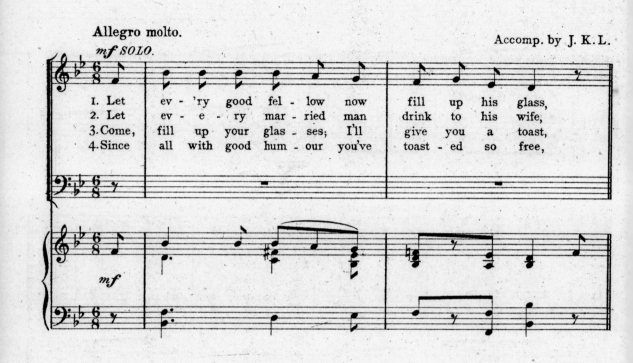

1. Let ev - 'ry good fel - low now fill up his glass,
2. Let ev - e - ry mar - ried man drink to his wife,
3. Come, fill up your glas - ses; I'll give you a toast,
4. Since all with good hum - our you've toast - ed so free,

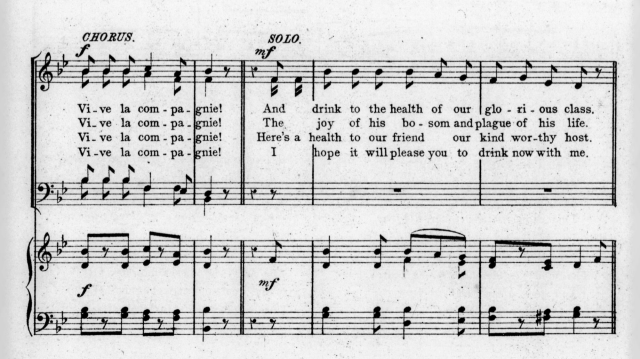

Vi - ve la com - pa - gnie! And drink to the health of our glo - ri - ous class.
Vi - ve la com - pa - gnie! The joy of his bo - som and plague of his life.
Vi - ve la com - pa - gnie! Here's a health to our friend our kind wor - thy host.
Vi - ve la com - pa - gnie! I hope it will please you to drink now with me.

I CANNOT EATE BUT LYTYLL MEATE.

Words from the Comedy
"Gammer Gurton's Needle." (1575?)

Allegretto.

Arr. by W. H. M.

i. I can-not eate but
ii. I love noo roste but

ly-tyll meate my stomacke ys not goode but sure I thyncke that I cowde dryncke with
a browne toste or a crabbe in the fyer a ly-tyll breade shall do me steade mooche

hym that werythe an hoode thowthe I goo bare take yow no care I am nothynge
breade I neuer de-syer dryncke ys my lyfe al-thowgthe my wyfe some tyme do chyde and

colde I stuffe my skynne so full with-in of jo-ly goode ale and olde.
scolde yete spare I not to plye the potte of jo-ly goode ale and olde.

CHORUS.

backe and syde goo bare goo bare bothe hande and fote goo colde but
backe and syde goo bare goo bare bothe hande and fote goo colde but

bel - ly god sende the goode | ale | in-owghe whe-ther | hyt be newe or | olde.___
bel - ly god sende the goode | ale | in-owghe whe-ther | hyt be newe or | olde.___

D.C. al Segno.

iii.   & yf that I
      may have trwly
goode ale my belly full
    I shall looke lyke one
    by swete sainte johnn
were shoron agaynste the woole
    nor froste nor snowe
    nor wynde I trow
canne hurte me yf hyt wolde
    I am so wrapped
    within & lapped
with joly goode ale & olde.
    backe & syde &c.

iv.   I care ryte nowghte
    I take no thowte
for clothes to kepe me warme
    have I goode dryncke
    I surely thyncke
nothynge canne do me harme
    for trwly than
    I fear no man
be he neuer so bolde
    when I am armed
    & throwly warmed
with joly goode ale & olde.
    backe & syde &c.

v.   but nowe & than
    I curse & banne
they make ther ale so small
    god geve them care
    & evill to fuare
they strye the malte & all
    sooche pevisshe pewe
    I tell yowe trwe
not for a crovne of golde
    ther commethe one syppe
    within my lyppe
whether hyt be newe or olde.
    backe & syde &c.

vi.   goode ale & stronge
    makethe me amonge
full joconde & full lyte
    that ofte I slepe
    & take no kepe
frome mornyng vntyll nyte
    then starte I vppe
    & fle to the cuppe
the ryte waye on I holde
    my thurste to staunche
    I fyll my paynche
with joly goode ale & olde.
    backe & syde &c.

vii.   & kytte my wyfe
    that as her lyfe
lovethe well goode ale to seke
    full ofte drynkythe she
    that ye maye se
the tears ronne downe her cheke
    then dothe she troule
    to me the bolle
as a goode malte worme sholde
    & saye swete harte
    I have take my parte
of joly goode ale & olde.
    backe & syde &c.

viii.   then let vs dryncke
    tyll we nodde and wyncke
even as goode fellowes shulde do
    we shall notte mysse
    to have the blysse
that goode ale dothe brynge men to
    & all poore soules
    that skowre blacke bolles
& them hathe lustely trowlde
    god save the lyves
    of them & ther wyves
whether they be yonge or olde.
    backe & syde &c.

CONCERNING I AND NON-I.

German Volkslied, "Seit Vater Noah."
Arr. by J. K. L.

Words by Prof. John Stuart Blackie.

1. Since Fa - ther No - ah first tapp'd the vine, And warm'd his jol - ly old
2. The po - ets, God knows, a jo - vial race, Have ev - er been laud-ing of
3. But I, who quaff the thought - ful well Of Pla - to and old Ar - is -

nose,____ All men to drink - ing do much in - cline, But
wine;____ Of Bac - chus they sing, and his ro - sy face, And the
to - tle, And Kant and Fich - te and He - gel, can tell The

why, no drink - er yet knows. We drink, and we nev - er think how!
draught of the beak - er di - vine; Yet all their fine phras-es are vain;
wis - dom that lies in the bot - tle; I drink, and in drink-ing I know:

CHORUS.

And yet, in our drink-ing, The root of deep think-ing Lies ve-ry profound, As
They pour out the es-sence Of brain-ef-fer-ves-cence, With rhyme and rant And
With glance keen and nim-ble I pierce thro' the sym-bol, And seize the soul Of

I will ex-pound To all who will drink with me now!
jing-ling cant, But no-thing at all they ex-plain.
truth in the bowl Be-hind the mere sen-su-ous show!

4.

Now brim your glass, and plant it well
Beneath your nose on the table,
And you will find what philosophers tell
Of I and non-I is no fable.
Now listen to wisdom, my son!
    Myself am the subject,
    This wine is the object,
    These things are two,
    But I'll prove to you
That subject and object are one.

5.

I take this glass in my hand, and stand
Upon my legs, if I can,
And look and smile benign and bland,
And feel that I am a man.
Now stretch all the strength of your brains!
    I drink – and the object
    Is lost in the subject,
    Making one entity,
    In the identity
Of me and the wine in my veins!

6.

And now if Hamilton, Fraser, or Mill,
This point can better explain,
You may learn from them with method and skill,
To plumb the abyss of your brain;
But this simple faith I avow,
    The root of true thinking
    Lies just in deep drinking,
    As I have shown
    In a way of my own,
To this jolly good company now.

THE LITTLE BROWN JUG.

Allegretto.

R. A. Eastburn.

1. My wife and I liv'd all a-lone, In a lit-tle log-hut we call'd our own;
2. 'Tis you who make my friends my foes, 'Tis you who make me wear old clothes;

She lov'd gin, and I lov'd rum,– I tell you what, we'd lots of fun.
Here you are, so near my nose, So tip her up and down she goes.

CHORUS.

Ha, ha, ha, you and me, "Lit - tle brown jug," don't
I love thee, Ha, ha, ha, you and me,
"Lit - tle brown jug," don't I love thee.

3.
When I go toiling to my farm,
  I take little "Brown Jug" under my arm;
I place it under a shady tree,
  Little "Brown Jug" 'tis you and me. *Chorus.*

4.
If all the folks in Adam's race,
  Were gather'd together in one place;
Then I'd prepare to shed a tear,
  Before I'd part from you, my dear. *Chorus.*

5.
If I'd a cow that gave such milk,
  I'd clothe her in the finest silk;
I'd feed her on the choicest hay,
  And milk her forty times a day. *Chorus.*

6.
The rose is red, my nose is, too,
  The violet's blue, and so are you;
And yet I guess before I stop,
  We'd better take another drop. *Chorus.*

CRAMBAMBULI.

Translated from the German of Crescentius Koromandel (1745)
by Prof. John Stuart Blackie.

German Folk-Air of the 18th Century.

Cram - bam - bu - li, that is the li - quor, That fires the blood, makes
My pan - a - ce - a's in the bea - ker, For ev - 'ry ill that

bright the brains, Tra - li - ra! At morn-ing bright, at noon, at night, Cram-
earth con - tains, Tra - li - ra!

bam-bu - li is my de-light, Cram - bim - bam - bam - bu - li, Cram - bam - bu - li!

CRAMBAMBULI.

Translated from the German of Crescentius Koromandel (1745)
by Prof. John Stuart Blackie.

German Folk-Air of the 18th Century.

1.

Crambambuli, that is the liquor
  That fires the blood, makes bright the brains,
    Tra-li-ra!
My panacea's in the beaker,
  For ev'ry ill that earth contains,
    Tra-li-ra!
At morning bright, at noon, at night,
Crambambuli is my delight.
    Crambimbambambuli, Crambambuli.

2.

When on the road mine host receives me
  Like some great lord or cavalier,
    Tra-li-ra!
No fuming roast or boil deceives me,
  "What, garçon, ho! – the cork-screw here!"
    Tra-li-ra!
Then blows the guard his taranti,
To my good glass Crambambuli,
    Crambimbambambuli, Crambambuli.

3.

When queasy qualms torment me sadly,
  As some vile imp my soul possessed;
    Tra-li-ra!
When heaped distempers goad me madly,
  Colds in my head, coughs in my breast–
    Tra-li-ra!
Sir Doctor, devil take your drugs!
Why, don't you see our merry mugs
    Bright with Crambambuli, Crambambuli.

4.

Were I the Kaiser Maximilian,
  A noble order in the land,
    Tra-li-ra!
I'd make, and write in bright vermilion
  This motto on a silver band–
    Tra-li-ra!
"Toujours fidèle et sans souci,
C'est l'ordre de Crambambuli,
    Crambimbambambuli, Crambambuli."

5.

When to my pay my purse is debtor,
  By bowls and billiards cleaned out quite;
    Tra-li-ra!
When brings the post a black-sealed letter,
  Or my dear girl forgets to write;
    Tra-li-ra!
I drink, from sheer *melancholie,*
A little glass Crambambuli,
    Crambimbambambuli, Crambambuli.

6.

Whoso at us Crambambulisten
  Proudly turns up his churlish nose,
    Tra-li-ra!
He is a heathen and no Christian,
  For God's best gift away he throws;
    Tra-li-ra!
The fool may bawl himself to death.
I will not give, to stop his breath,
    One drop Crambambuli! Crambambuli!!!

Recipe for Crambambuli. "Take two bottles of light porter or ale, and boil them in a pan. Then put in half a pint of rum or arrac, and from half a pound to a pound of loaf-sugar. After this has boiled for a few minutes, take from the fire, and put into the mixture the white and the yellow of from six to eight eggs, previously whisked properly into one homogeneous mass. Then stir the whole for a minute or two, fill into a punch-bowl, and drink out of tumblers. It tastes equally well cold or hot."

WEIN, WEIB, GESANG.

(Wine, Woman and Song.)

Words by Carl Müchler. (1802.)
Translation by John Addington Symonds.

Air by Carl Friedrich Zelter. (1802.)
Arr. by W. H. M.

1. Der Wein er-freut des
1. Oh! wine it glads the

Men - schen Herz, Drum gab uns Gott den Wein! Auf! lasst bei Re - ben -
heart of man: There - fore God gave us wine! Ho, lads! fill high the

saft und Scherz Uns un - ser's Da - seins freun! Wer sich er - freut thut
flow - ing can: Let mirth and youth com - bine! Men light of heart per -

sei - ne Pflicht, Drum sto - sset an und sin - get dann, Was
form life's part: Then up and drink! Sing, while you drink, What

Mar - tin Lu - ther spricht, Was Mar - tin Lu - ther spricht:
Mar - tin Lu - ther saith, What Mar - tin Lu - ther saith:

CHORUS.

"Wer nicht liebt Wein, Weib und Ge - sang, Der bleibt ein Narr sein
"Who loves not wo - man, wine and song, He bides a fool his

Le - ben lang." Und Nar - ren sind wir nicht! Nein, Nar - ren sind wir nicht!
whole life long." And fools we are not, no! Nay, fools we are not, no!

D. C. al Segno.

2.

Die Lieb' erhebt des Menschen Herz
  Zu schöner Edelthat,
Schafft Linderung für jeden Schmerz,
  Streut Licht auf dunkeln Pfad.
Weh' dem, dem Lieb' und Wein gebricht!
  Drum küsst und trinkt, klingt an und singt,
Was Martin Luther spricht: Chorus.

3.

Ein Lied voll reiner Harmonie
  In treuer Freunde Kreis,
Ist Labung nach des Tages Müh'
  Und nach der Arbeit Schweiss.
Drum ruhet nach erfüllter Pflicht
Und klinget an und singet dann,
  Was Martin Luther spricht: Chorus.

2.

Oh, love it lifts the heart of man
  To deeds of noble worth;
Love softens every care, and can
  Shed light of heaven on earth!
Without or wine or love men pine:
  Then kiss and drink! Sing, while you drink,
  What Martin Luther saith: *Chorus.*

3.

A tuneful song, a jolly lay,
  Sung 'mid good companies,
Brings comfort at the close of day,
  And after labour ease.
Rest then at last, now work is past!
Your glasses clink; sing while you drink,
  What Martin Luther saith: *Chorus.*

TABLE-SONG.

Words by Wolfgang von Goethe (1802.)
Translation by Edward Oxenford.

Music by Max Eberwein, (1810.)

1. *Mich ergreift, ich weiss nicht wie,*
   Himmlisches Behagen.
   Will mich's etwa gar hinauf
   Zu den Sternen tragen?
   Doch ich bleibe lieber hier,
   Kann ich redlich sagen,
   Beim Gesang und Glase Wein
   Auf den Tisch zu schlagen.

2. *Wundert euch, ihr Freunde, nicht,*
   Wie ich mich geberde;
   Wirklich ist es allerliebst
   Auf der lieben Erde;
   Darum schwör' ich feierlich
   Und ohn' alle Fährde,
   Dass ich mich nicht freventlich
   Wegbegeben werde.

3. *Da wir aber allzumal*
   So beisammen weilen,
   Dächt' ich, klänge der Pokal
   Zu des Dichters Zeilen.
   Gute Freunde ziehen fort,
   Wohl ein hundert Meilen,
   Darum soll man hier am Ort
   Anzustossen eilen.

4. *Lebe hoch, wer Leben schafft!*
   Das ist meine Lehre.
   Unser König denn voran,
   Ihm gebührt die Ehre.
   Gegen in - und äussern Feind
   Setzt er sich zur Wehre;
   An's Erhalten denkt er zwar,
   Mehr noch, wie er mehre.

5. *Nun begrüss' ich sie sogleich,*
   Sie die einzig Eine.
   Jeder denke ritterlich
   Sich dabei die Seine.
   Merket auch ein schönes Kind,
   Wen ich eben meine,
   Nun so nicke sie mir zu:
   Leb' auch so der Meine!

6. *Freunden gilt das dritte Glas,*
   Zweien oder dreien,
   Die mit uns am guten Tag
   Sich im stillen freuen,
   Und der Nebel trübe Nacht
   Leis' und leicht zerstreuen;
   Diesen sei ein Hoch gebracht
   Alten oder Neuen.

7. *Breiter wallet nun der Strom*
   Mit vermehrten Wellen;
   Leben jetzt im hohem Ton,
   Redliche Gesellen!
   Die sich mit gedrängter Kraft
   Brav zusammen stellen
   In des Glückes Sonnenschein
   Und in schlimmen Fällen.

1. O'er me steal, I know not how,
   Thoughts as bright as heaven.
   Would they bear me to the stars,
   Whence such thoughts are given?
   Here I rather would remain
   Long as I am able,
   Fill the glass and sing a strain,
   Rap the laden table!

2. Think not I am strange, my friends,
   Lost my senses rightful,
   When I say this dear old earth,
   Truly is delightful!
   Therefore I make solemn vow,—
   Pass it or receive it,—
   Ne'er, till I to fate must bow,
   Will I strive to leave it!

3. As we sit assembled here,
   Gay and joyous-hearted,
   Oft I think how poets quaffed
   In the days departed.
   Friends to distant regions go,
   Leagues o'er hills and heather,
   Let us then, our thoughts to show,
   Glasses clink together!

4. Long live he who life makes safe!
   That's my honest notion.
   So unto the king who rules
   Pledge your hearts' devotion,
   'Gainst all foes, afar or near,
   He is ever striving;
   Holding all his country dear,
   Sure defeat contriving.

5. Then to her, the only one,
   I the glass am raising,
   So do all of you, my friends,
   Each his own one praising!
   Should a maiden fair to see;
   Sweet, and angered never,
   Look this way and smile on me,
   May she live for ever!

6. Friends partake of glasses three,
   Ne'er the senses cloying;
   Happy then indeed are we,
   Wine and wit enjoying.
   When the hour grows late, and some
   Homeward must be wending,
   Then a toast for them shall come,
   Blithe be their off-sending.

7. Wider flows the stream of wit
   As the night progresses;
   Life is excellent like this,
   Everyone confesses!
   Troublous thoughts fly far away,
   Bright ones twine together,
   All enjoy while here they stay,
   Life's divinest weather!

TABLE-SONG.

Words by Wolfgang von Goethe. (1802.)
Translation by Edward Oxenford.

Music by Max Eberwein (1810.)

Mich ergreift, ich weiss nicht wie, Himmlisches Be-ha-gen. Will mich's et-wa gar hinauf
O'er me steal, I know not how, Thoughts as bright as heav-en. Would they bear me to the stars,

zu den Ster-nen tra-gen? Doch ich blei-be lie-ber hier, Kann ich red-lich sa-gen,
Whence such thoughts are giv-en? Here I ra-ther would remain Long as I am ab-le,

D. S. for Chorus.

Beim Ge-sang und Gla-se Wein Auf den Tisch zu schla-gen.
Fill the glass and sing a strain, Rap the la-den ta-ble!

8.

Wie wir nun beisammen sind,
Sind zusammen viele.
Wohl gelingen denn, wie uns,
Andern ihre Spiele!
Von der Quelle bis an's Meer
Mahlet manche Mühle,
Und das Wohl der ganzen Welt
Ist's, worauf ich ziele.

8.

E'en as we our glasses clink,
  Others so are clinking,
May their hearts be gay as ours,
  Ours their way of thinking!
'Twixt the birth hour and the end
  Pleasures rise before us,
Grasp them, then, I urge each friend,
  While their spell is o'er us!

HERR BRUDER, NIMM DAS GLÄSCHEN.

(Come, brothers, fill your glasses.)

Folk Song, known in 1810.
Translation by Edward Oxenford.

German Folk Melody, (1810.)

1.

Herr Bruder, nimm das Gläschen
Und trink' es fröhlich aus!
Und wirbelt's dir im Näschen,
So bring' ich dich nach Haus.
Bedenk', es ist ja morgen
Schon alles wieder gut;
Der Wein vertreibt die Sorgen
Und macht uns frohen Muth.
Halli, hallo, halli, hallo,
Bei uns geht's immer so.

2.

Sind gleich jetzt Sorg' und Plage
Und manche Tyrannei
Begleiter unsrer Tage,
Das geht schon auch vorbei.
Die Hoffnung lacht von weiten,
Auf, fasset neuen Muth!
Es kommen bess're Zeiten,
Und alles wird noch gut! Chorus.

3.

Mach's nur wie ich, und denke:
'S ist doch die beste Welt!
Es gibt da ein Getränke,
Das unsern Muth erhält.
Und dieser Welt zum Lobe
Trinkt noch ein Glas rein aus
Bis auf die Nagelprobe;
Heut' kommt's auf Eins heraus! Chorus.

4.

Ja, diese Welt soll leben!
Ihr Sorgen, gute Nacht!
Hoch leb' der Saft der Reben,
Der uns so heiter macht!
Es leb' in unserm Städtchen
Ein jeder treue Freund;
Und hoch das brave Mädchen
Das es noch ehrlich meint! Chorus.

5.

Fest stehe, ohne Ende,
Der Freundschaft heil'ger Bund!
Drauf reichet euch die Hände
Zum Bruderkuss den Mund!
In trüb' und heitern Tagen
Woll'n wir mit deutscher Treu'
Als Brüder uns vertragen
Als Freunde stehen bei. Chorus.

6.

In diesem frohen Kreise,
Da trinkt sich's doppelt schön:
Man ist so recht im Gleise
Und lässt die Welt sich drehn.
Man füllt sein Glas auf's Neue
Mit Hoffnungsphantasie,
Stösst an und ruft mit Weihe:
Hoch leb' die Harmonie! Chorus.

1.

Come, brothers, fill your glasses
And drink the red wine up;
There's nought on earth surpasses
The cheerful, brimming cup!
No thought accord the morrow,
But live your lives to-day;
Good wine dispels all sorrow,
And courage gives alway!
Halli, hallo, halli, hallo!
With us 'tis ever so!

2.

If care should hover o'er you
And troubles spread their net,
Drink up the wine before you,
And soon you will forget!
Remember hope is shining
Like sunshine after rain;
Take courage, never pining,
Good times will come again! *Chorus.*

3.

Come, follow my example,
And vow the world is fair,
Our lot a famous sample
Of man's existence there!
This is a cure unfailing,
So shout it with a will;
When worries are assailing
'Twill all with courage fill! *Chorus.*

4.

Yes, long may be enduring,
This world of yours and mine,
To us the while securing
A glass of good red wine!
Long live our well-loved city,
And every faithful friend,
All maidens sweet and pretty
On whom our hearts depend! *Chorus.*

5.

Stand fast and true for ever
To Friendship's holy bond;
Refuse its right hand never,
But to its grasp respond!
In times of joy or sadness
Our steadfast faith we'll teach,
Yes, thro' all woe or gladness,
Stand firmly each by each! *Chorus.*

6.

At this our merry meeting
Each draught's an aid to joy;
Our mood is one that's greeting
Delight without alloy!
So fill the bumper, brothers,
Let Hope your comrade be;
Clink glasses each with others,
And sing "Live Harmony!" *Chorus.*

HERR BRUDER, NIMM DAS GLÄSCHEN.

(Come, brothers, fill your glasses.)

Folk Song, known in 1810.
Translation by Edward Oxenford.

German Folk-Melody, (1810.)

Herr Bru - der, nimm das Gläs - chen Und trink' es fröh - lich
Come, bro - thers, fill your glas - ses, And drink the red wine

aus! Und wir - belt's dir im Näs - chen, So
up; There's nought on earth sur - pas - ses The

bring' ich dich nach Haus Be - denk', es ist ja
cheer - ful, brim - ming cup No thought ac - cord the

mor - gen Schon al - les wie - der gut; Der
mor - row, But live your lives to - day! Good

Wein ver - treibt die Sor - gen Und macht uns fro - hen Muth.
wine dis - pels all sor - row, And cour - age gives al - way.

CHORUS.

Hal - li, hal - lo, hal - li, hal - lo! Bei uns geht's im - mer
Hal - li, hal - lo, hal - li, hal - lo! With us 'tis ev - er

so! Hal - li, hal - lo, hal - li, hal - lo! Bei uns geht's im - mer so!
so! Hal - li, hal - lo, hal - li, hal - lo! With us 'tis ev - er so!

DIVERS DITTIES.

"Chaos is come again".

Othello, iii. 3.

OVER THE SEA TO SKYE.

"The air, partly based on an old chanty, was composed by Annie C. McLeod, and is taken by permission from "Songs of the North" Cramer & Co., Ltd., London."

Words by Robert Louis Stevenson.

Arr. by W. Augustus Barratt.

Words printed by kind permission of Charles Baxter, Esq., for the Executors of the late Mr. Stevenson.

Sir Harold Boulton, owner of the Copyright of the air of the "Skye Boat Song" and author of the original words of this universally known song, has kindly allowed the use of the air in this book to the words Robert Louis Stevenson was afterwards inspired to write to the same air round Sir Harold's refrain of "Over the Sea to Skye."

YE BANKS AND BRAES.

Words by Robert Burns, (1792.)

Arr. by Sir Herbert Oakeley, Mus. Doc., &c.

From "Eighteen Scottish Melodies, arranged for Male chorus for the Universities of Scotland," and orchestrated for Edinburgh University Musical Society, by Sir Herbert Oakeley. Printed by his kind permission.

DIE LORELEI.

Words by Heinrich Heine.(1823.)
Translation by F. W. Farrar.

Music by Friedrich Silcher.
Arr. by W. Augustus Barratt.

Allegretto.

Ich weiss nicht was soll es be - deu - ten, dass
I know not why, but my glad - ness Hath

ich so trau - rig bin, _____ Ein Mär - chen aus al - ten
ut - ter - ly pass'd a - way, _____ And my spi - rit is fill'd to

Zei - ten, das kommt mir nicht aus dem Sinn. _____ Die
sad - ness With the lilt of an old - en lay. _____ The

Luft ist kühl und es dun - kelt, Und ru - hig fliesst der Rhein.____ Der
air is dew - y and dark - ling, And calm - ly flow-eth the Rhine;____ The

Gip - fel des Ber - ges fun - kelt Im A - bend-son - nen - schein.
crest of the hills is spark - ling In the ros-es of e - ven - shine.

2.

Die schönste Jungfrau sitzet
  Dort oben wunderbar,
Ihr goldnes Geschmeide blitzet,
  Sie kämmt sich ihr goldenes Haar.
Sie kämmt es mit goldenem Kamme
  Und singt ein Lied dabei,
Das hat eine wundersame
  Gewaltige Melodei.

3.

Den Schiffer im kleinen Schiffe
  Ergreift es mit wildem Weh;
Er sieht nicht die Felsenriffe,
  Er schaut nur hinauf in die Höh'.
Ich glaube, die Wellen verschlingen
  Am Ende noch Schiffer und Kahn;
Und das hat mit ihrem Singen
  Die Lorelei gethan.

2.

There sitteth a maid in the gloaming,
  A maiden divinely fair;
'Mid the gleam of her gems she is combing
  The curls of her golden hair.
From a golden comb she is raining
  Her tresses, and sings from on high,
A passionate, soul-enchaining,
  Invincible melody.

3.

The sailor, with wild pangs thrilling,
  Is chain'd by the magic tone;
The breakers his skiff are filling,
  But he gazeth on her alone.
Ah me! in the surge descending,
  He is swept with his little boat;
And such is ever the ending
  Of the Lorelei's witching note.

JOHN PEEL.

Arr. by John Tait.

With spirit.

1. D'ye ken John Peel with his coat so gay, D'ye ken John Peel at the
2. Yes, I ken John Peel and Ru - by too! Ran - ter and Ring - wood,
3. Then here's to John Peel from my heart and soul, Let's drink to his health, let's
4. D'ye ken John Peel with his coat so gay? He liv'd at Trout - beck

break of the day, D'ye ken John Peel when he's
Bell - man and True, From a find to a check, from a
fin - ish the bowl. We'll fol - low John Peel from thro'
once on a day; Now he has gone far,

far, far a - way, With his hounds and his horn in the morn - ing?
check to a view, From a view to a death in the morn - ing.
fair and thro' foul, If we want a good hunt in the morn - ing.
far, far, a - way; We shall ne'er hear his voice in the morn - ing.

CHORUS.

For the sound of his horn brought me from my bed, And the cry of his hounds which he oft - times led; Peel's view hal-loo would a - wak - en the dead, Or the fox from his lair in the morn - - ing.

A-HUNTING WE WILL GO.

Words by Henry Fielding. (1707 - 1754.)

English Air.
Arr. by W. Augustus Barratt.

Allegro con brio.

1. The dusk - y night rides down the sky, And ush - ers in the morn; The hounds all join in glo - rious cry, The hounds all join in glo - rious cry, The hunts - man winds his horn, The hunts - man winds his horn.

CHORUS.

Then a-hunt-ing we will go, will go, Then a-hunt-ing we will go, will go, A-

hunt-ing, hunt-ing we will go, A-hunt-ing we will go.

2.

The wife around her husband throws
　Her arms, and begs him stay;
"My dear, it rains, it hails, it snows,
　You will not hunt to-day?"
　　But a-hunting we will go, etc.

3.

"A brushing fox in yonder wood,
　Secure to find we seek;
For why, I carried, sound and good,
　A cart-load there last week.
　　And a-hunting we will go, etc.

4.

Away he goes, he flies, the rout
　Their steeds all spur and switch;
Some are thrown in, and some thrown out,
　And some thrown in the ditch.
　　But a-hunting we will go, etc.

5.

At length, his strength to faintness worn,
　Poor Reynard ceases flight;
Then, hungry, homeward we return,
　To feast away the night.
　　Then a-drinking we do go, etc.

DRINK, PUPPY, DRINK.

Hunting Song.

Words and Music by G. J. Whyte-Melville.*

Arr. for Male Voices by J. K. L.

Moderato.

Here's to the fox in his earth below the rocks! And here's to the line that we fol-low, And here's to the hound with his nose up-on the ground, Tho' merri-ly we whoop and we holloa!

2.

Here's to the horse, and the rider too, of course;
And here's to the rally o' the hunt, boys;
Here's a health to every friend, who can struggle to the end,
And here's to the Tally-ho in front, boys. *Chorus.*

3.

Here's to the gap, and the timber that we rap,
Here's to the white thorn, and the black, too;
And here's to the pace that puts life into the chase,
And the fence that gives a moment to the pack, too. *Chorus.*

4.

Oh! the pack is staunch and true, now they run from scent to view,
And it's worth the risk to life and limb and neck, boys;
To see them drive and stoop till they finish with "Who-whoop,"
Forty minutes on the grass without a check, boys. *Chorus.*

* By permission of Messrs. Chappell & Co., 50 New Bond Street, London.

CHORUS.

Then drink, pup-py, drink, and let ev'-ry pup-py drink, That is old e-nough to lap and to swallow, For he'll grow in-to a hound, So we'll pass the bot-tle round, And mer-ri-ly we'll whoop and we'll hol-loa.

THE HUNTER'S LIFE.

Words by Wilhelm Bornemann (1816).
Translation by Edward Oxenford.

Folk-Melody (Von Gehricke?)(1827).

1. Im Wald und auf der Hei - de, Da such' ich mei - ne Freu - de, Ich bin ein Jä - gers-mann, Ich bin ein Jä - gers - mann. Den Wald und Forst zu he - gen, Das Wild-pret zu er - le - gen, Mein' Lust hab' ich dar an,_ Mein' Lust hab' ich dar - an._ Hal - li,_ hal - lo, hal - li,_ hal - lo, Mein' Lust hab' ich dar - an._ Hal - li,_ hal - lo, hal - li,_ hal - lo, Mein' Lust hab' ich dar - an._

1. A - mid the woods and hea - ther, All heed-less of the wea - ther, I roam, a hun - ter free, I roam, a hun - ter free!_ To see the co - verts thriv - ing, The game to cap - ture striv - ing, A plea-sure is to me,_ A plea-sure is to me!_ Hal - li,_ hal - lo, hal - li,_ hal - lo, A plea - sure is to me,_ Hal - li,_ hal - lo, hal - li,_ hal - lo, A plea - sure is to me!_

CHORUS.

* A good effect is got by playing the first three lines of accompaniment for right hand an octave lower.

THE HUNTER'S LIFE.

Words by Wilhelm Bornemann (1816).
Translation by Edward Oxenford.

Folk-Air (Von Gehricke?),(1827.)

1.

Im Wald und auf der Heide,
Da such' ich meine Freude,
Ich bin ein Jägersmann!
Den Wald und Forst zu hegen,
Das Wildpret zu erlegen,
Mein' Lust hab' ich daran!
Halli! Hallo!

I.

Amid the woods and heather,
All heedless of the weather,
I roam, a hunter free!
To see the coverts thriving,
The game to capture striving,
A pleasure is to me!
Halli! Hallo!

2.

Trag' ich in meiner Tasche
Ein Trünklein in der Flasche,
Zwei Bissen liebes Brod;
Brennt lustig meine Pfeife,
Wenn ich den Forst durchstreife,
Da hat es keine Noth.

2.

Within my pouch, quite handy,
I keep some wine or brandy,
Of bread a goodly store!
My pipe serenely smoking,
While pleasant thoughts invoking,
I wish for nothing more!

3.

Im Walde hingestrecket,
Den Tisch mit Moos mir decket
Die freundliche Natur;
Den treuen Hund zur Seite
Ich mir das Mahl bereite
Auf Gottes freier Flur.

3.

Upon the sward reclining,
Of mosses intertwining,
I there a table make.
Then of my meal so sparing,
My good dog with me sharing,
I gratefully partake.

4.

Das Huhn im schnellen Zuge,
Die Schnepf' im Zickzackzuge
Treff' ich mit Sicherheit;
Die Sauen, Reh' und Hirsche
Erleg' ich auf der Birsche,
Der Fuchs lässt mir sein Kleid.

4.

The hawk, when skyward hieing,
The snipe, when zigzag flying,
I never fail to hit!
The stag, and boar that rushes,
I slay amid the bushes,
And foxes I outwit.

5.

Und streich' ich durch die Wälder,
Und zieh' ich durch die Felder
Einsam den ganzen Tag;
Doch schwinden mir die Stunden
Gleich flüchtigen Secunden,
Tracht' ich dem Wilde nach.

5.

As 'midst the woods I wander,
Or over fields meander,
I'm lone the whole day through.
But hours pass soon and brightly,
And press on me but lightly,
Whilst I the game pursue!

6.

Wenn sich die Sonne neiget,
Der feuchte Nebel steiget,
Mein Tagwerk ist gethan,
Dann zieh' ich von der Heide
Zur häuslich stillen Freude,
Ein froher Jägersmann!

6.

At eve, when fall the shadows,
And mists enshroud the meadows,
I lay my weapons by.
Then gath'ring up my treasures,
I wend to homely pleasures,—
A happy hunter I!

THE VICAR OF BRAY.

Words about 1720.

Air — 17th Century.
Arr. by John Tait.

Marcato *(Symphony before first verse only.)*

1. In good King Charles's golden days, When loy-al-ty no harm meant, A zea-lous High Church-
2. When roy-al James obtained the crown, And Pop'ry came in fa-shion, The pe-nal laws I

man was I, And so I got pre-fer-ment; To teach my flock I nev-er missed, Kings
hoot-ed down, And read the De-clar-a-tion; The Church of Rome I found would fit Full

were by God ap-point-ed, And damn'd are those who do re-sist, Or touch the Lord's a-noint-ed.
well my con-sti-tu-tion; And had become a Je-su-it, But for the Re-vo-lu-tion.

CHORUS.

And this is law, that I'll main-tain, Un-til my dy-ing day, sir, That

what-so-ev-er King shall reign, I'll be the Vi-car of Bray, sir.

3.

When William was our King declared,
  To ease the nation's grievance,
With this new wind about I steered,
  And swore to him allegiance;
Old principles I did revoke,
  Set conscience at a distance;
Passive obedience was a joke,
  A jest was non-resistance. *Chorus.*

4.

When gracious Anne became our Queen,
  The Church of England's glory,
Another face of things was seen,
  And I became a Tory;
Occasional Conformists base,
  I damn'd their moderation,
And thought the Church in danger was
  By such prevarication. *Chorus.*

5.

When George in pudding-time came o'er,
  And moderate men looked big, sir,
I turned a cat-in-pan once more,
  And so became a Whig, sir;
And thus preferment I procured
  From our new faith's defender,
And almost every day abjured
  The Pope and the Pretender. *Chorus.*

6.

The illustrious house of Hanover,
  And Protestant succession,
To these I do allegiance swear,—
  While they can keep possession;
For in my faith and loyalty
  I never more will falter,
And George my lawful King shall be—
  Until the times do alter. *Chorus.*

THE OLD SCOTTISH CAVALIER.

Words by William Edmondstoune Aytoun, D.C.L.*

Air.—"The old Scottish Cavalier."
Arr. by W.H.M.

I. Come list-en to an-o-ther song, Should make your heart beat high, Bring the crim-son to your fore-head And the lus-tre to your eye. It is a song of old-en time, Of days long since gone by,___ And of a ba-ron stout and bold As e'er wore sword on thigh!___ And

CHORUS.

Like a brave old Scot-tish Ca-va-lier, All of the old-en time!

2.

He kept his castle in the north,
  Hard by the thundering Spey;
And a thousand vassals dwelt around,
  All of his kindred they.
And not a man of all that clan
  Had ever ceased to pray
For the Royal race they loved so well,
  Though exiled far away
    From the steadfast Scottish Cavaliers,
    All of the olden time!

3.

His father drew the righteous sword
  For Scotland and her claims,
Among the loyal gentlemen
  And chiefs of ancient names,
Who swore to fight or fall beneath
  The standard of King James,
And died at Killiecrankie Pass
  With the glory of the Græmes;
    Like a true old Scottish Cavalier,
    All of the olden time!

4.

He never owned the foreign rule,
  No master he obeyed,
But kept his clan in peace at home,
  From foray and from raid;
And when they asked him for his oath,
  He touched his glittering blade,
And pointed to his bonnet blue,
  That bore the white cockade:
    Like a leal old Scottish Cavalier,
    All of the olden time!

5.

At length the news ran through the land—
  THE PRINCE had come again!
That night the fiery cross was sped
  O'er mountain and through glen;
And our old baron rose in might,
  Like a lion from his den,
And rode away across the hills
  To Charlie and his men,
    With the valiant Scottish Cavaliers,
    All of the olden time!

6.

He was the first that bent the knee
  When the Standard waved abroad,
He was the first that charged the foe
  On Preston's bloody sod;
And ever, in the van of fight,
  The foremost still he trod,
Until on bleak Culloden's heath,
  He gave his soul to God,
    Like a good old Scottish Cavalier,
    All of the olden time!

7.

Oh! never shall we know again
  A heart so stout and true—
The olden times have passed away
  And weary are the new:
The fair white rose has faded
  From the garden where it grew,
And no fond tears, save those of heaven,
  The glorious bed bedew
    Of the last old Scottish Cavalier,
    All of the olden time!

THE POACHER.

Old English.

Arr. by W. Augustus Barratt.

Heartily.

1. When I was bound ap-pren-tice, in fa-mous Lincoln-shire,— Full well I serv'd my mas-ter for more than se-ven year,— Till I took up to poaching, as you shall quicki-ly hear; Oh, 'tis my de-light on a shin-ing night, in the sea-son of the year!—

2.

As me and my companions were setting of a snare,
'Twas then we spied the gamekeeper – for him we did not care,
For we can wrestle and fight, my boys, and jump o'er anywhere. *Chorus.*

3.

As me and my companions were setting four or five,
And taking on 'em up again, we caught a hare alive,
We took the hare alive, my boys, and through the woods did steer. *Chorus.*

4.

I threw him on my shoulder, and then we trudgéd home,
We took him to a neighbour's house and sold him for a crown,
We sold him for a crown, my boys, but I did not tell you where. *Chorus.*

5.

Success to every gentleman that lives in Lincolnshire,
Success to every poacher that wants to sell a hare,
Bad luck to every gamekeeper that will not sell his deer. *Chorus.*

KING ARTHUR.

Dorsetshire Ballad.

Air founded on
"In Good old Colony Times."
Arr. by J. K. Lees.

1. King Ar-thur ruled the land, that he did. And a right good ru-ler was he, that he was. He had three sons of yore, and he kick'd them to the door, Be-cause they would not sing,

CHORUS in Unison.

Be-cause they would not sing, Be-cause they would not sing, He had three sons of yore, and he kick'd them to the door, Be-cause they would not sing.

2.
The first he was a miller— that he was;
The second he was a weaver— that he was;
And the third he was a little tailor boy,
With his broad-cloth under his arm.

3.
The miller he stole corn— that he did;
The weaver he stole yarn— that he did;
And the little tailor boy he stole corduroy
To keep the other fellows warm.

4.
The miller he was drowned in his dam— that he was;
The weaver he was hanged with his yarn— that he was;
But the devil ran away with the little tailor boy,
With the broad-cloth under his arm.

WHEN THE KING ENJOYS HIS OWN AGAIN.

Song of the Cavaliers
in the reign of Charles I.

Traditional Air, 17th Century.
Arr. by John Tait.

I.

Let rogues and cheats prognosticate
Concerning Kings or kingdom's fate,
I think myself to be as wise
As he that gazeth on the skies;
 My sight goes beyond
 The depth of a pond,
Or rivers in the greatest rain;
 Whereby I can tell
 That all will be well
When the King enjoys his own again.
Chorus. Yes, this I can tell,
  That all will be well,
  When the King enjoys his own again.

2.

There's neither swallow, dove, nor dade,
Can soar more high or deeper wade;
Nor show a reason from the stars
What causeth peace or civil wars;
 The man in the moon
 May wear out his shoon
By running after Charles his wain;
 But all's to no end,
 For the times will not mend
Till the King enjoys his own again. *Chorus.*

3.

Full forty years this royal crown
Hath been his father's and his own;
And is there any one but he
That in the same should sharer be?
 For who better may
 The sceptre sway
Than he that hath such right to reign?
 Then let's hope for a peace,
 For the wars will not cease
Till the King enjoys his own again. *Chorus.*

4.

Though for a time we see Whitehall
With cobwebs hanging on the wall,
Instead of gold and silver brave,
Which formerly 'twas wont to have,
 With rich perfume
 In every room,
Delightful to that princely train;
 Yet the old again shall be
 When the time you see
That the King enjoys his own again. *Chorus.*

5.

Then fears avaunt! upon the hill
My hope shall cast her anchor still,
Until I see some peaceful dove
Bring home the branch I dearly love;
 Then will I wait
 Till the waters abate
Which now disturb my troubled brain;
 Then for ever rejoice
 When I've heard the voice
That the King enjoys his own again. *Chorus.*

WHEN THE KING ENJOYS HIS OWN AGAIN.

Song of the Cavaliers
in the reign of Charles I.

Traditional Air, 17th Century.
Arr. by John Tait.

Let rogues and cheats prog - nos - ti - cate Con - cern - ing King's or king - dom's fate, I think my - self to be as wise As he that gaz - eth on the skies; My sight goes be - yond The

depth of a pond, Or riv - ers in the great - est rain; Where-

by I can tell That all will be well, When the king en - joys his own a - gain.

CHORUS.

Yes, this I can tell, That all will be well, When the king en - joys his own a - gain.

SIMON THE CELLARER.

Words by W. H. Bellamy.

Music by J. L. Hatton.

Allegretto.

1. Old Si - mon the Cel - lar - er keeps a rare store, Of Malm - sey and Mal - voi -
2. Dame Mar - ge - ry sits in her own still-room, And a ma - tron sage is
3. Old Si - mon he sits in his high - back'd chair, And talks a - bout tak - ing a

sie, _____ And Cy - prus, and who can say how ma - ny more? For a
she; _____ And thence oft at Cur - few is waft - ed a fume, She
wife; _____ And Mar - ge - ry of - ten is heard to de - clare, She

CAKES AND ALE.

Words by Dr. A. Stodart Walker.

Music by Dr. de Clive Lowe.

Tempo di Valse.

Andante ma non troppo.

1. The heart may be sad in its hey — day, The glow of life seem to pale, And yet if it's wint — ry on May — day There still will be cakes and ale. Let's laugh when the heart is ach — ing, Let's dance when our hope doth

2. We're in the blush of our noon — day, Think not of our eve — ning pale; When grub-bing for bread and but — ter, Gives place to cakes and ale. Mope not though time ring the chang — es, We'll find the breeze for the

cres. poco a poco   *rall. molto*

fail; There's a time for sleep and for wak - ing, For du - ty and cakes and
sail; Though to-mor-row to du - ty ran - ges, To-day we have cakes and

ale.

Tempo di Valse.

Cakes and ale, cakes and ale Life has no count of jots or tit-tles; Yet cakes and

ale will some-time fail. Life is not all beer and skittles. Cakes and ale,

cakes and ale, Life has no count of jots or tit - tles; Yet cakes and ale will

234

some-time fail, Life is not all beer and skit-tles.

3. We'll think when our locks are whit - en'd, When we

near the end of our tale, Of the days when du - ty was light - en'd By

eve - nings of cake and ale, By eve - nings of cake and ale.

FUNICULI, FUNICULA.

Words by Edward Oxenford.

Music by L. Denza.

Allegretto brillante.

1. Some think _____ the world is made for fun and fro - lic, _____ And so do I! _____
2. Some think _____ it wrong to set the feet a - danc - ing, _____ But not so I! _____
3. Ah me! _____ 'tis strange that some should take to sigh - ing, _____ And like it well! _____

NB. This song can be sung with or without chorus.
Included by arrangement with Messrs. G. Ricordi & Co., Milan.

238

* 2nd verse: Music sounds afar, etc. 3rd verse: Hark, the soft guitar, etc.

SHERLOCK HOLMES.

Words and Music by Claude Ralston.

1. I would in-dite this dit-ty to a man who's ve-ry cute, He's the ter-ror of Bill Sloggins and them who'd do a scoot; He can tell you where you've been to just by looking at your boot, And you'll know him by the name of Sher-lock Holmes. With his

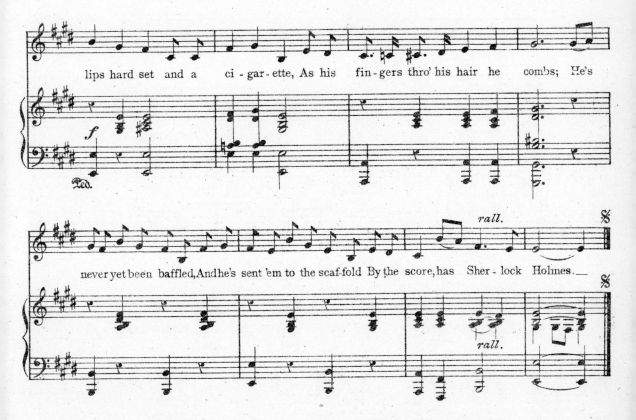

lips hard set and a ci - gar - ette, As his fin - gers thro' his hair he combs; He's

never yet been baffled, And he's sent 'em to the scaffold By the score, has Sher - lock Holmes.

2.

I asked him out to dine at my place near Kempton Park,
I said the wine was Ruinart, I'd shifted every mark;
"You lie! it's three-and-sixpenny, I know it by the cork,
    For I've found it on the floor," said Sherlock Holmes. *Chorus.*

3.

One summer day we started for a race-course close to town,
He said "against the favourite," we planked our utmost "brown,"
And before that race was over, why, the favourite he broke down,—
    "That physic's done the trick," said Sherlock Holmes. *Chorus.*

4.

He asked a few pals up one night; at Poker we did play;
The stakes were high, the end drew nigh,–this great man was no jay–
Five aces on the table, with a pistol, he did lay,—
    "I shall now collect the oof," said Sherlock Holmes. *Chorus.*

5.

You say it is a pity that this splendid man should die.
I think the Swiss tale is a plant, I'll give my reason why.
There's a lady in the question, so he's gone and done a "guy,"
    But he'll turn up again, will Sherlock Holmes.
      With his lips hard set and his cigarette,
      As his fingers thro' his hair he combs;
      He's never yet been baffled,
      And he'll send 'em to the scaffold
      By the score, will Sherlock Holmes.

OLD KING COLE.

he, Then twee-twee-dle-dee, twee-dle-dee, tweedle-dee, then twee-twee-dle-dee, twee-dle-

dee went the fid-dlers. And so mer-ry we'll all be.

2.

Old King Cole was a merry old soul,
    And a merry old soul was he,
He called for his pipe and he called for his bowl,
    And he called for his pipers three.
Ev'ry piper he had a fine pipe,
    A very fine pipe had he,
Then tootle-tootle-too, tootle-too went the pipers.
    And so merry, merry we'll all be.

3.

Old King Cole was a merry old soul,
    And a merry old soul was he,
He called for his pipe and he called for his bowl,
    And he called for his harpers three.
Ev'ry harper he had a fine harp,
    A very fine harp had he,
Then twang, twang-a-twang, twang-a-twang went the harpers.
    And so merry, merry we'll all be.

4.

Old King Cole was a merry old soul,
    And a merry old soul was he,
He called for his pipe and he called for his bowl,
    And he called for his drummers three.
Ev'ry drummer he had a fine drum,
    A very fine drum had he,
Then rub, rub-a-dub, rub-a-dub went the drummers.
    And so merry, merry we'll all be.

ABDUL, THE BULBUL AMEER.

Con spirito.

Music by "Ali Baba."

1. The sons of the Pro-phet are hard-y and bold, And quite un-ac-cus-tom'd to fear;— But of all, the most reck-less of life or of limb, Was Ab-dul, the Bul-bul A-meer.— When they want-ed a man to en-cour-age the van, Or to shout "hull-a-loo" in the rear,— Or to storm a re-doubt, they

By special permission of Mr. John Blockley, 16 Mortimer Street, London, W.

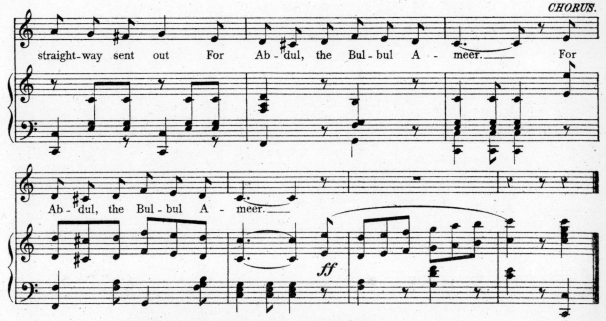

straight-way sent out For Ab - dul, the Bul - bul A - meer.____ For

Ab - dul, the Bul - bul A - meer.____

ff

2. There are heroes in plenty and well-known to fame
   In the ranks that are led by the Czar;
   But among the most reckless of name or of fame
   Was Ivan Petruski Skivah.
   He could imitate Irving, play euchre or pool,
   And perform on the Spanish guitar;
   In fact, quite the cream of the Muscovite team
   Was Ivan Petruski Skivah.

3. One morning the Russian had shouldered his gun
   And put on his most cynical sneer,
   When, going down town, he happened to run
   Into Abdul, the Bulbul Ameer.
   Said the Bulbul, "Young man, is your life then so dull,
   That you're anxious to end your career?
   For, infidel, know that you've trod on the toe
   Of Abdul, the Bulbul Ameer."

4. Said the Russian, "My friend, your remarks in the end
   Will only prove futile, I fear;
   For I mean to imply that you're going to die,
   Mr. Abdul, the Bulbul Ameer."
   The Bulbul then drew out his trusty chibouque,
   And, shouting out "Allah Aklar,"
   Being also intent upon slaughter, he went
   For Ivan Petruski Skivah.

5. When, just as the knife was ending his life –
   In fact, he had shouted "Huzza!"–
   He found himself struck by that subtle calmuck,
   Bold Ivan Petruski Skivah.
   There's a grave where the wave of the blue Danube flows,
   And on it, engraven so clear,
   Is, "Stranger, remember to pray for the soul
   Of Abdul, the Bulbul Ameer."

6. Where the Muscovite maiden her vigil doth keep
   By the light of the true lover's star,
   The name she so tenderly murmurs in sleep
   Is "Ivan Petruski Skivah."
   The sons of the Prophet are hardy and bold;
   And quite unaccustomed to fear;
   But, of all, the most reckless of life or of limb,
   Was Abdul, the Bulbul Ameer.

THE MASSACRE OF MACPHERSON.

A Highland Legend
(from the Gaelic.)

Words from "The Bon Gaultier Ballads."

1. Oh! Fhair-shon swore a feud A - gainst ta clan Mac - Ta - vish,

March'd in - to their land To mur - der and to ra - vish;

For he did re - solve To ex - tir - pate ta fi - pers, With

four and twen - ty men, And five and thir - ty pi - pers. Oh!

CHORUS. *)
Ee

SOLO. Ta-a-a-a-a. Ta-a-a-a-a-a. Ta-a-a-a-a. An' t'at's ta Gae-lic cho-rus.
Ah

Oom

*) Both Solo and Chorus must be sung in a droning, nasal manner.

THE MASSACRE OF MACPHERSON.

1.

Oh! Fhairshon swore a feud
  Against ta clan Mac-Tavish,
March'd into their land
  To murder and to ravish;
For he did resolve
  To extirpate ta fipers,
With four and twenty men,
  And five and thirty pipers. Oh!
    Chorus.

2.

But when he had gone
  Half-way down Strath Canaan,
Of his fighting tail
  Just three were remainin';
They were all he had
  To back him in ta battle,
All the rest had gone
  Off to drive ta cattle.
    Chorus.

3.

"Fery coot!" cried Fhairshon,
  "So my clan disgraced is;
Lads, we'll need to fight
  Pefore we touch ta peasties.
Here's Mhic-Mac-Methuselah
  Comin' wi his fassals,
Ghillies seventy-three
  And sixty Dhuine-wassails."
    Chorus.

4.

"Coot tay to you, sir;
  Are you not ta Fhairshon?
Was you comin' here
  To fisit any person?
You're a plackguard, sir!
  It is now six hundred
Coot long years, and more,
  Since my glen was plundered."
    Chorus.

5.

"Fat is tat you say?
  Dare you cock your peaver?
I will teach you, sir,
  Fat is coot pehaviour!
You shall not exist
  For another day more;
I will shoot you, sir,
  Or stap you with my claymore."
    Chorus.

6.

"I am fery glad
  To learn what you mention,
Since I can prevent
  Any such intention."
So Mhic-Mac-Methuselah
  Gave some warlike howls,
Trew his skhian-dhu,
  An' stuck it in his powels.
    Chorus.

7.

In this fery way
  Tied ta faliant Fhairshon,
Who was always thought
  A most superior person.
Fhairshon had a son
  Who married Noah's daughter,
And nearly spoiled ta flood
  By trinking up ta water.
    Chorus.

8.

Which he would have done—
  I, at least, believe it—
Had ta mixture peen
  Only half Glenlivet.
This is all my tale;
  Sirs, I hope 'tis new t'ye.
Here's your fery coot healths,
  And tamn ta whusky duty!
    Chorus.

Words included by kind permission of Messrs. Wᵐ Blackwood and Sons, Edinburgh, publishers of "The Bon Gaultier Ballads."

COCK ROBIN.

Arr. for Male voices.
With accomp. by J. K. L.

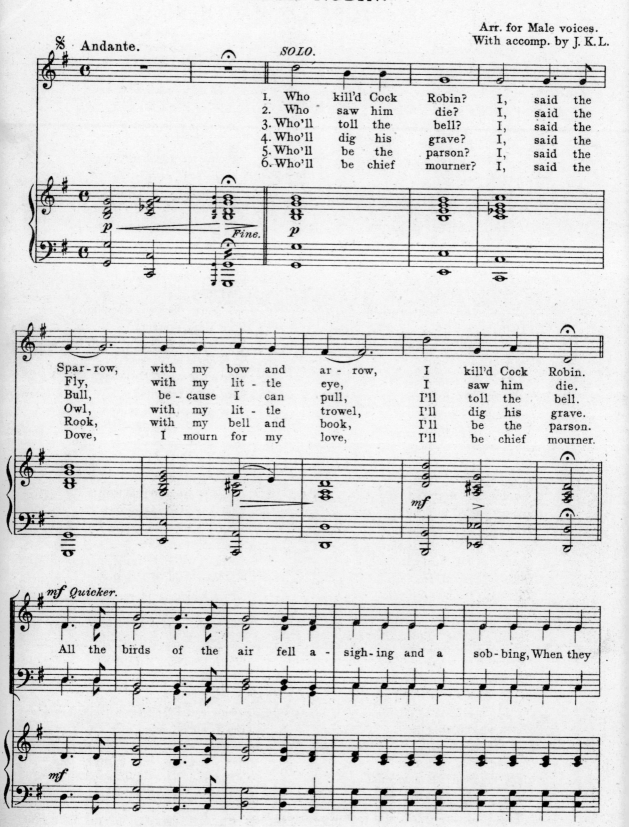

JINGLE, BELLS.

J. Pierpont.

1. Dash - ing thro' the snow, In a one - horse o - pen sleigh,
2. A day or two a - go, I thought I'd take a ride, And
3. Now the ground is white; Go it while you're young,

O'er the fields we go, Laugh - ing all the way;
soon Miss Fan - nie Bright Was seat - ed by my side. The
Take the girls to - night, And sing this sleigh - ing song. Just

Bells on bob - tail ring, Mak - ing spi - rits bright; What
horse was lean and lank; Mis - for - tune seemed his lot; He
get a bob - tailed bay, Two - for - ty for his speed; Then

fun it is to ride and sing A sleigh - ing song to - night!
got in - to a drift - ed bank, And we, we got up - sot.
hitch him to an o - pen sleigh, And crack! you'll take the lead.

CHING-A-LING.

BARITONE SOLO.

1. We re-vel in song; to Spain we be-long,
2. We charm and en-trance all men in the dance,

CHORUS.

La, la, la, la, la, la, la, la, la, la, la, la,

Far o'er the o-cean. When Lu-ci-fer's star Shines clear in the east, we re-
Come they from near us or come they from far; We dance and we glide, while

La, la, la, la, la, la, la, la, la, la, la, la, la, la, la, la, la, la,

turn from the feast, To the tune of our light gui-tar. Ha! Ha!
loud far and wide, Sounds the tune of our light gui-tar. Ha! Ha!

la, la, la, la, la, la, la, la, la, la, la, la, la, la. Ha! Ha!

CHORUS.

Ching - a - ling - a - ling, ching - a - ling - a - ling, Ha, ha, ha, ha!

Ching - a - ling - a - ling, ching - a - ling - a - ling, Ha, ha, ha, ha!

These were the words which we heard from a - far. Ching - a - ling - a - ling, ching - a - ling - a - ling,

These were the words which we heard from a - far. Ching - a - ling - a - ling, ching - a - ling - a - ling,

Ha, ha, ha, ha! To the tune of our light gui - tar. Ha, ha!

Ha, ha, ha, ha! To the tune of our light gui - tar. Ha, ha!

THE SPANISH GUITAR.

Adapted by W. J. H. and J. E. J.

1. When I was a stu-dent at Ca-diz, _____ I

played on the Span-ish gui-tar, ching, ching! I used to make love to the

la - dies, _____ I think of them still from a - far, ching, ching!

CHORUS. *Accompaniment same as for Solo.*

Tra la la la, tra la la la, tra la la la,

Ring, ching, ching! Ring, ching, ching! Ring out, ye

Tra la la la, tra la la la, tra la la la,

tra la la la, tra la la la, Tra la la la,

bells, Oh ring out, ye bells, Oh

tra la la la, tra la la la, Tra la la la,

2.

I was four years a student at Cadiz,
  Where nothing one's pleasure can mar, ching, ching!
And where many a beautiful maid is,
  Oh I strumm'd and I twang'd my guitar, ching, ching!

3.

Oh I sang serenades there at Cadiz,
  Till I got an attack of catarrh, ching, ching!
Though no more I could serenadize,
  Still I played on my Spanish guitar, ching, ching!

4.

When at last the train bore me from Cadiz,
  The ladies all wept round the car, ching, ching!
Oh it grieved me to part from those ladies,
  But I carried away my guitar, ching, ching!

5.

I'm no longer a student at Cadiz,
  But I play on the Spanish guitar, ching, ching!
And still I am fond of the ladies,
  Though now I'm a happy papa, ching, ching!

THE SPANISH CAVALIER.

Words and Music by W. D. Hendrickson.

CHORUS.

Say, dar-ling, say, when I'm far a-way Some-times you may think of me, dear; Bright sun-ny days will soon fade a-way, Re-mem-ber what I say, and be true, dear.

LISTEN TO MY TALE OF WOE.

Words by Eugene Field.

Melody by Hubbard T, Smith.

Moderato.

1. A lit-tle peach in an or-chard grew,___ List-en to my tale of
2. Now up at the peach a club they threw;___ List-en to my tale of
3. Un-der the turf where the dai-sies grew,___ List-en to my tale of
4. Up thro' the turf where they laid them two,___ List-en to my tale of

woe,___ A lit-tle peach of em-'rald hue,
woe,___ Down from the limb on which it grew,
woe,___ They plant-ed John and his sis-ter Sue,
woe,___ There sprang a tree of a kind we knew, And

Warm'd by the sun and wet by the dew, It grew, It
Fell the lit-tle peach of em-'rald hue,___ Poor John! Poor
And their lit-tle souls to the an-gels flew,___ Boo-hoo! Boo-
soon through its branch-es the ze-phyrs blew, A-whoo! A-

CHORUS.
With spirit.

Hard tri - als for them two, John - ny Jones and his

sis - ter Sue, And the peach of em - 'rald hue,

grew, That grew,
That grew, That grew, List-en to my tale of woe.

UPIDEE.

Various versions of the words of this song are current— all of them parodies of Longfellow's "Excelsior," five verses of which are here inserted.

Fine.

D. S. al Fine.

2.

His brow was sad, his eye beneath
Flashed like a falchion from its sheath,
And like a silver clarion rung
The accents of that unknown tongue. *Chorus.*

3.

"O stay," the maiden said, "and rest
Thy weary head upon my breast."
A tear stood in his bright blue eye,
But still he answered with a sigh. *Chorus.*

4.

At break of day as heavenward
The pious monks of Saint Bernard
Uttered the oft-repeated prayer,
A voice cried through the startled air. *Chorus.*

5.

A traveller, by the faithful hound,
Half buried in the snow was found,
Still grasping in his hand of ice
That banner with the strange device. *Chorus.*

THERE IS A TAVERN IN THE TOWN.

Adapted from a Cornish Folksong.

1. There is a tav-ern in the town, in the town, And there my dear love sits him down, sits him down, And drinks his wine 'mid laugh-ter free, And nev-er, nev-er thinks of me.

2. He left me for a dam-sel dark, dam-sel dark, Each Fri-day night they used to spark, used to spark, And now my love, once true to me, Takes that dark dam-sel on his knee.

3. Oh! dig my grave both wide and deep, wide and deep, Put tomb-stones at my head and feet, head and feet, And on my breast carve a tur-tle dove, To sig-ni-fy I died of love.

CHORUS.

Fare thee well, for I must leave thee, Do not let the part-ing grieve thee, And re-

mem-ber that the best of friends must part, must part. A-

dieu, a-dieu, kind friends, a-dieu, a-dieu, a-dieu, I can no long-er stay with

a - dieu, a - dieu, a - dieu, I can no long - er

you, stay with you. I'll hang my harp on a weep-ing wil-low tree, And

may the world go well with thee.

may the world, the world go well with thee, go well with thee.

thee.

thee, go well with thee.

MUSH, MUSH.

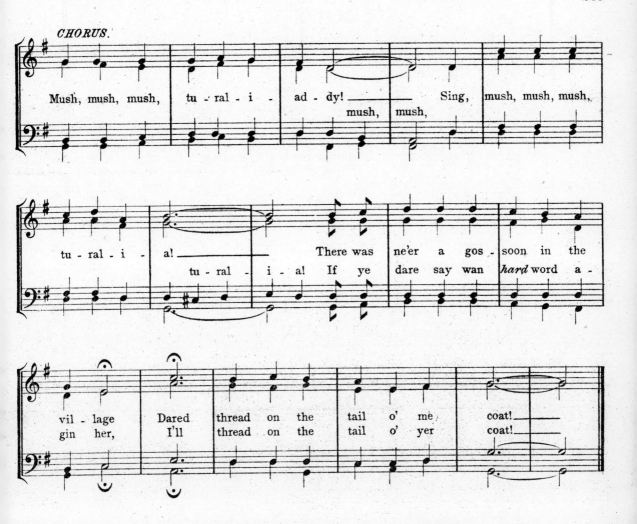

CHORUS.

Mush, mush, mush, tu-ral-i-ad-dy! ___ mush, mush, Sing, mush, mush, mush, tu-ral-i-a! ___ tu-ral-i-a! If ye There was ne'er a gos-soon in the dare say wan *hard* word a-

vil-lage Dared thread on the tail o' me, coat! ___
gin her, I'll thread on the tail o' yer coat! ___

3.

But a blackguard, called Mickey Maloney,
 Came an' sthole her affictions away;
Fur he'd money an' I hadn't ony,
 So I sint him a challenge nixt day.
In the ayvenin' we met at the Woodbine,
 The Shannon we crossed in a boat;
An' I lathered him wid me shillaly,
 Fur he throd on the tail o' me _ *Chorus.*

4.

Oh, me fame wint abroad through the nation,
 An' folks came a-flockin' to see;
An' they cried out, widout hesitation _
 "You're a fightin' man, Billy Mc Gee!"
Oh, I've claned out the Finnigan faction,
 An' I've licked all the Murphys afloat;
If you're in fur a row or a raction,
 Jist ye thread on the tail o' me _ *Chorus.*

SOLOMON LEVI.

Allegretto.

Words and Music by Fred Seaver.

1. My name is Sol-o-mon Le-vi; at my store on Chat-ham
2. And if a bum-mer comes a-long to my store on Chat-ham

Street, That's where you'll buy your coats and vests, and ev'-ry-thing that's
Street, And tries to hang me up for coats and vests so ve-ry

neat; I've se-cond-hand-ed ul-sterettes, and ev'-ry-thing that's
neat; I kicks the bummer right out of my store, and on him sets my

fine, For all the boys they trade with me at a hun-dred and for-ty-
pup, For I won't sell clothing to a-ny man who tries to set me

nine. O Sol-o-mon Le-vi! Le-vi! tra la la la!
up.

CHORUS in unison

Poor Sheen-y Le-vi, Tra la la la la la la la la la. My

CHORUS.

name is Sol-o-mon Le-vi; at my store on Chat-ham Street, That's

where you'll buy your coats and vests, and ev'-ry-thing else that's neat; tra la la.

Se-cond-hand-ed ul-ster-ettes and ev'-ry-thing else that's fine; For

all the boys they trade with me at a hun-dred and for-ty-nine. *D. C.*

3.

The people are delighted to come inside of my store,
And trade with the elegant gentleman what I keeps to walk the floor.
He is a blood among the Sheenies, beloved by one and all,
And his clothes they fit him just like the paper on the wall. *Chorus.*

THE THREE CROWS.

2.

Said one old crow unto his mate,
   Chorus. O Billy Magee Magar! } *(bis.)*
Said one old crow unto his mate,
  "What shall we do for grub to ate?" *Chorus.*

3.

"There lies a horse on yonder plain,"
   Chorus. O Billy Magee Magar! } *(bis.)*
"There lies a horse on yonder plain,
  Who's by some cruel butcher slain." *Chorus.*

4.

"We'll perch ourselves on his backbone,"
   Chorus. O Billy Magee Magar! } *(bis.)*
"We'll perch ourselves on his backbone,
  And pick his eyes out one by one." *Chorus.*

5.

"The meat we'll eat before it's stale,"
   Chorus. O Billy Magee Magar! } *(bis.)*
"The meat we'll eat before it's stale,
  Till nought remain but bones and tail." *Chorus.*

COCKLES AND MUSSELS.

Music by James Yorkston.

Andante.

1. In Dub-lin's fair ci - ty, Where the girls are so pret - ty, I
2. She was a fish - mong-er, But sure 'twas no won - der, For
3. She died of a fe - ver, And no one could save her, And

first set my eyes on sweet Mo - ly Ma - lone, As she wheel'd her wheel-
so were her fa - ther and mo - ther be - fore, And they each wheel'd their
that was the end of sweet Mol - ly Ma - lone; But her ghost wheels her

1-3. barrow Thro' streets broad and nar-row, Cry-ing, Cockles and mussels! a - live, a-live, O!

CHORUS.

A - live, a - live, O! A - live, a - live,

O! Cry-ing, Cock - les and mus - sels! a - live, a - live, O!

CANNIBALEE.

Words by G. H. M.

Music by M. A. Taylor.

Moderato.

1. There lived a young maid on a can-ni-bal isle, She was fair-er than fair could be; No sweet-er young sa-vage had ev-er been born, Her eyes were as bright as the star of the morn, And her teeth were as sharp as the point of a thorn: She was won-drous fair to see!

2. There came to the is-land from o-ver the main, A mar-i-ner bold and free; He looked on the maiden with ma-ny a sigh, And he whis-pered, "My dar-ling, my I of mine I, You must love me and wed me, or else I must die." 'Twas a woe-ful sight to see.

3. And the maid-en re-plied with a can-ni-bal smile, "I a-dore thee, O thee of my thee: There's no-thing I love like a lust-y young wit, Just cooked to a mo-ment and fresh from the spit; And I'll eat you all up to the ve-ry last bit, Your dar-ling young canni-bal-ee!

Bass Voices.

1. So she was.
2. So it was.
3. Canniba-lee.

RIDING DOWN FROM BANGOR.

Arr. by S. E. Farwell.

2. Emp-ty seat be-hind him, No one at his side,
4. Pleas-ant-ly they chat-ted, How the cin-ders fly!
6. Out in-to the day-light Glides that east-ern train,

In-to qui-et vil-lage, East-ern train did glide. En-ter a-ged
Till the stu-dent fel-low Gets one in his eye.. Maid-en, sym-pa-
Stu-dent's hair is ruf-fled, Just the mer-est grain, Maid-en seen all

cou-ple, Take the hind-most seat, En-ter vil-lage maid-en,
thet-ic, Turns her-self a-bout, "May I, if you please, sir,
blush-es- When then and there ap-peared, A ti-ny lit-tle ear-ring, In that

Beau-ti-ful, pe-tite.
Try to get it out?"
hor-rid stu-dent's beard.

DEAR EVELINA, SWEET EVELINA.

thee shall nev-er, nev-er die. Dear Ev-e-li-na,

sweet Ev-e-li-na, My love for thee shall nev-er, nev-er die.

3.

Evelina and I, one fine evening in June,
Took a walk all alone by the light of the moon,
The planets all shone, for the heavens were clear,
And I felt round the heart most tremendously queer. *Chorus.*

4.

Three years have gone by, and I've not got a dollar;
Evelina still lives in that green grassy holler.
Although I am fated to marry her never,
I've sworn that I'll love her for ever and ever. *Chorus.*

ROSALIE.

Arr. by W. H. M.

2.

I'm *Pierre de Bonton de Paris, de Paris,*
I'm called by *les dames très joli, très joli,*
When I ride out each day in my little *coupé,*
I tell you I'm something to see. *Chorus.*

3.

I go to the *fête de Marquise, de Marquise,*
I go and make love at my ease, at my ease,
I go to her *père* and demand for my own,
The hand of my sweet Rosalie. *Chorus.*

CLEMENTINE.

Tempo di Mazurka.

Words and Music by Percy Montrose.

1. In a cav - ern, in a can - yon Ex - ca - vat - ing for a
2. Light she was and like a fai - ry, And her shoes were num - ber
3. Drove she duck - lings to the wa - ter Ev' - ry morn - ing just at

mine, Dwelt a min - er, for - ty - nin - er, And his daugh - ter Cle - men - tine.
nine; Her - ring - box - es, with - out top - ses, San - dals were for Cle - men - tine.
nine; Hit her foot a - gainst a splin - ter, Fell in - to the foam - ing brine.

CHORUS. *Accompaniment same as for Solo.*

Oh my dar - ling, Oh my dar - ling, Oh my dar - ling Cle - men -
Cle - men - tine, Cle - men - tine, Cle - men - Cle - men -

tine, Thou art lost and gone for ev - er, Dread - ful sor - ry, Clemen - tine.
tine, Clemen - Cle - men - tine, Clemen - tine, Clementine, Clemen - Clemen - tine.
Oh Clementine, Oh Clemen - Clemen - tine.

4.
Saw her lips above the water
  Blowing bubbles mighty fine;
But alas! I was no swimmer,
  So I lost my Clementine. *Chorus.*

5.
In a corner of the churchyard,
  Where the myrtle boughs entwine,
Grow the roses in their posies
  Fertilised by Clementine. *Chorus.*

6.
Then the miner, forty-niner,
  Soon began to peak and pine;
Thought he "oughter jine" his daughter.
  Now he's with his Clementine. *Chorus.*

7.
In my dreams she still doth haunt me,
  Robed in garments soaked in brine;
Though in life I used to hug her,
  Now she's dead I'll draw the line. *Chorus.*

8.
How I missed her, how I missed her,
  How I missed my Clementine!
But I kissed her little sister,
  And forgot my Clementine. *Chorus.*

BLOW THE MAN DOWN.

TRAMP! TRAMP! TRAMP! THE BOYS ARE MARCHING.

Tempo di marcia.

G. F. Root.

1. In the pri-son cell I sit, Think-ing, Mo-ther dear, of you, And our

bright and hap-py home so far a-way, And the tears they fill my eyes, Spite of

all that I can do, Tho' I try to cheer my com-rades and be gay.

Tramp, tramp, tramp, the boys are march-ing, Cheer up, com-rades, they will come; And be-

neath our country's flag We shall breathe the air a-gain, Of the freeland in our own be-lov-ed home.

2.

In the battle front we stood,
When their fiercest charge they made,
And they swept us off, a hundred men or more,
But before we reach'd their lines
They were beaten back dismay'd,
And we heard the cry of vict'ry o'er and o'er.
Tramp, tramp, tramp, the boys are marching,
Cheer up, comrades, they will come,
And beneath our country's flag
We shall breathe the air again,
Of the freeland in our own beloved home.

Tramp, tramp, tramp, etc.

3.

So within the prison cell,
We are waiting for the day
That shall come to open wide the iron door,
And the hollow eye grows bright,
And the poor heart almost gay,
As we think of seeing home and friends once more
Tramp, tramp, tramp, the boys are marching,
Cheer up, comrades, they will come,
And beneath our country's flag
We shall breathe the air again,
Of the freeland in our own beloved home.

Tramp, tramp, tramp, etc.

WHEN JOHNNY COMES MARCHING HOME.

March time.

Arr. by J. K. L.

SOLO.

The men will cheer, the boys will shout, The la-dies they will all turn out;
The vil-lage lads and lass-es say With ros-es they will strew the way;
The lau-rel-wreath is rea-dy now, To place up-on his roy-al brow;
And let each one per-form his part, To fill with joy the war-rior's heart;

CHORUS.

And we'll all feel gay When John-ny comes march-ing

home, And we'll all feel gay When John-ny comes march-ing home.

CHEER! BOYS, CHEER!

Words by Charles Mackay, LL. D.

Music by Henry Russell.

SOLO.

So fare - well, Eng - land, much as we may love thee,
Here we had toil and lit - tle to re - ward it, But

We'll dry the tears that we have shed be - fore.
there shall plen - ty smile up - on our pain; And

Why should we weep to sail in search of for - tune? So
ours shall be the prai - rie and the for - est, And

fare - well, Eng - land, fare - well for ev - er - more!
bound - less mea - dows ripe with gold - en grain.

286

Plantation Songs.

"They held opinion that the sweetness
of music did recreate the spirits, and
the heart did undertake to love."

SIR ANTONIE OF GUEVARA, *Familiar Epistles.*

OLD FOLKS AT HOME.

Words and Music by Stephen C. Foster.

Moderato.

1. 'Way down up-on de Swa-nee Rib-ber, Far, far a-way,
2. All round de lit-tle farm I wandered When I was young;
3. One lit-tle hut a-mong de bushes, One dat I love,

Dere's where my heart is turn-ing eb-ber: Dere's where de old folks stay.
Den ma-ny hap-py days I squandered, Ma-ny de songs I sung.
Still sad-ly to my mem'-ry rush-es, No mat-ter where I rove.

All up and down de whole cre-a-tion, Sad-ly I roam,
When I was play-ing wid my brud-der, Hap-py was I.
When shall I see de bees a-humming, All round de comb?

Still long-ing for de old plan-ta-tion, And for de old folks at home.
Oh! take me to my kind old mud-der; Dere let me lib and die.
When shall I hear de ban-jo thrumming, Down in my good old home?

CHORUS.

All de world am sad and drea-ry, Eb'-ry-where I roam. O darkeys, how my

heart grows wea-ry, Far from de old folks at home.

POOR OLD JOE.

Poco Adagio.

Words and Music by Stephen C. Foster.

1. Gone are the days when my heart was young and gay,
2. Why should I weep when my heart should feel no pain?
3. Where are the hearts once so hap-py and so free,

Gone are my friends from the cot-ton fields a-way, Gone from the earth to a
Why do I sigh that my friends come not a-gain, Griev-ing for forms now de-
The children so dear that I held up-on my knee? Gone to the shore where my

bet-ter land I know,
part-ed long a-go? } I hear their gen-tle voi-ces call-ing "Poor old Joe."
soul has long'd to go;

CHORUS.

I'm coming, I'm coming, For my head is bending low, I hear their gentle voices calling "Poor old Joe."

19

GOOD OLD JEFF.

Arr. by J. K. L.

1. 'Tis just a year a-go to-day, That I re-mem-ber well; I sat down by poor Nel-ly's side, And a sto-ry she did tell,_____ 'Twas a-bout a poor old

2. She took my arm, we walk'd a-long, In-to an o-pen field; And then she paus'd to breathe a while, Then to his grave did steal._____ She sat down by that

3. But since that time how things are chang'd! Poor Nell, that was my bride, Is laid be-neath the cold grave-sod, Down by her fa-ther's side._____ I plant-ed there up-

MASSA'S IN DE COLD GROUND.

Words and Music by Stephen C. Foster.

1. Round de mea-dows am a-ring-ing,
2. When de au-tumn leaves were fall-ing,
3. Mas-sa make de dark-eys love him,

dark-eys' mourn-ful song,
When de days were cold,
'Cause he was so kind;

While de mock-ing-bird am
'Twas hard to hear ole mas-sa
Now dey sad-ly weep a-

sing-ing,
call-ing,
bove him,

Hap-py as de day am
'Cause he was so weak and
Mourn-ing 'cause he leave dem

long.
old.
behind.

Where de i-vy am a creep-ing,
Now de o-range tree am bloom-ing,
I can-not work be-fore to-mor-row,

I'SE GWINE BACK TO DIXIE.

Allegretto.

Not too fast.

Melody by C. A. White.

1. I'se gwine back to Dix-ie, No more I'se gwine to wan-der; My
2. I've hoed in fields of cot-ton, I've work'd up-on the riv-er; I
3. I'm trav'-ling back to Dix-ie; My step is slow and fee-ble; I

heart's turn'd back to Dix-ie, I can't stay here no long-er. I
used to think if I got off I'd go back there, no nev-er. But
pray the Lord to help me, And lead me from all e-vil. And

miss de ole plan-ta-tion, My home and my re-la-tion, My
time has chang'd the old man, His head is bend-ing low, His
should my strength for-sake me, Then, kind friends, come and take me, My

ad lib.

heart's turn'd back to Dix-ie, And I must go.
heart's turn'd back to Dix-ie, And he must go.
heart's turn'd back to Dix-ie, And I must go.

colla voce

CHORUS.

Ise gwine back to Dix-ie, I'se gwine back to Dix-ie, I'se gwine where the or-ange blos-soms grow; For I hear the chil-dren call-ing, I see their sad tears fall-ing; My heart's turn'd back to Dix-ie, And I must go.

UNCLE NED.

Written and Composed by Stephen C. Foster.

Accomp. and arr. for Male Voices by J. K. L.

SOLO.

There was an old nig-ger, and his name was Un-cle Ned, But he's dead long a-go, long a-

go; He had no wool on de top of his head, In de

place where the wool ought to grow. Den lay down de shubble an' de

hoe, _____ Hang up de fid-dle an' de bow.

CHORUS.
p

Dere's no more hard work for poor old Ned, He's gone whar de good nig-gers go,

Dere's no more hardwork for poor old Ned, He's gone whar de good nig-gers go.

2.

His fingers were long as de cane in de brake,
  He had no eyes for to see,
He had no teeth for to eat de corn-cake,
  So he had to let de corn-cake be.
    Den lay down de shubble an' de hoe, etc.

3.

When old Ned die Massa take it mighty hard,
  De tears run down like de rain;
Old Missus turn pale, an' she get berry sad,
  Cayse she nebber see old Ned again.
    Den lay down de shubble an' de hoe, etc.

OLD CABIN HOME.

Arr. for Male voices,
with accomp. by J. K. L.

Moderato.

1. I am go-ing far a-way, far a-
2. I am going to leave this land, with
3. When old age is com-ing on, and my

way to leave you now, To the Mis-sis-sip-pi ri-ver I am
all this dar-key band, All the wide world o-ver to
hair is turn-ing gray, I will hang up the ban-jo all a-

going; And I'll take my old ban-jo, and I'll
roam; But when I'm tired and weary, I will
lone; And to pass the time a-way, I will

sing this lit-tle song, 'Way down in my old ca-bin home.
lay me down to rest 'Way down in my old ca-bin home.
sit down by the fire, 'Way down in my old ca-bin home.

CHORUS *a little slower.*

Down in my old ca-bin home, There lies my sis-ter and my bro-ther,

There lies my wife, she was the joy of my life, And the child in the grave with its mo-ther.

Tempo. After last verse.

Di-nah, don't you go, Di-nah, don't you go, Down to the banks of the O - hi - o,

Di-nah, don't you go, Di-nah, don't you go, Down to the O - hi - o.

MARCHING THROUGH GEORGIA.

Words and Music by Henry C. Work.

Tempo di marcia.

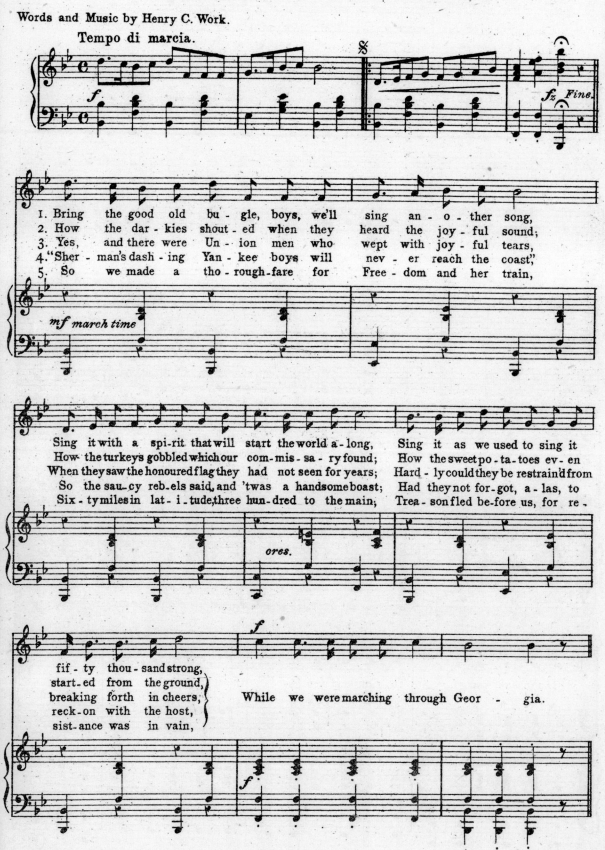

1. Bring the good old bu - gle, boys, we'll sing an - o - ther song,
2. How the dar - kies shout - ed when they heard the joy - ful sound;
3. Yes, and there were Un - ion men who wept with joy - ful tears,
4. "Sher - man's dash - ing Yan - kee boys will nev - er reach the coast,"
5. So we made a tho - rough - fare for Free - dom and her train,

Sing it with a spi - rit that will start the world a - long, Sing it as we used to sing it
How the turkeys gobbled which our com - mis - sa - ry found; How the sweet po - ta - toes ev - en
When they saw the honoured flag they had not seen for years; Hard - ly could they be restrain'd from
So the sau - cy reb - els said, and 'twas a handsome boast; Had they not for - got, a - las, to
Six - ty miles in lat - i - tude, three hun - dred to the main; Trea - son fled be - fore us, for re -

fif - ty thou - sand strong,
start - ed from the ground,
breaking forth in cheers,
reck - on with the host,
sist - ance was in vain,

While we were marching through Geor - gia.

CHORUS.

KINGDOM COMING.

Words and Music by Henry C. Work.

CHORUS.

mf De mas - sa run? ha, ha! De dark - eys stay? ho, ho! It

cres. mus' be now de king - dom com - in', An' de year ob Ju - bi - lo!

rall.

3.

De darkeys feel so lonesome, libing
    In de log-house on de lawn,
Dey move dar tings to massa's parlour,
    For to keep it while he's gone.
Dar's wine an' cider in de kitchen,
    An' de darkeys dey'll hab some;
I spose dey'll all be confiscated
    When de Linkum sojers come. *Chorus.*

4.

De oberseer he make us trouble,
    An' he dribe us round a spell;
We lock him up in de smoke-house cellar,
    Wid de key trown in de well.
De whip is lost, de han'-cuff broken,
    But de massa'll hab his pay;
He's ole enough, big enough, ought to known better,
    Dan to went an' run away. *Chorus.*

WHO'S THAT CALLING?

Moderato.

Words and Music by J. B. Lawreen.

1. The moon is beam-ing o'er the spark-ling rill, Who's that a-
2. The leaves are rust-ling 'neath the star-lit sky, Who's that a-

call-ing? The flow'rs are sleep-ing on the plain and hill, Who's that call-ing so
call-ing? The stream-let mur-murs as it pass-es by, Who's that call-ing so

sweet? While the birds are rest-ing till the gold-en dawn, Who's that a-call-ing? 'Twas
sweet? Oh! is it a message from far o'er the sea, Who's that a-call-ing? Is

like the sing-ing of the one now gone, Who's that call-ing so sweet?
it my dar-ling who now speaks to me, Who is call-ing so sweet?

CHORUS.

Who's that a - call-ing? Who's that a - call-ing? Is it one we long to greet? _____ Who's that a - call-ing?

Who's that a - call-ing? Who's that a - call-ing so sweet? _____

POLLY-WOLLY-DOODLE.

fay! ____ Oh I'm off to Loui - si - an - a, for to

see my Su - sy An - na, Sing - ing "Pol - ly-wol - ly-doo-dle" all the day!

3.

Oh! I came to a river, an' I couldn't get across,
  Sing "Polly-wolly-doodle," all the day,
An' I jumped upon a nigger, for I thought he was a hoss,
  Sing "Polly-wolly-doodle," all the day. *Chorus.*

4.

Oh! a grasshopper sittin' on a railroad track,
  Sing "Polly-wolly-doodle," all the day,
A pickin' his teef wid a carpet tack,
  Sing "Polly-wolly-doodle," all the day. *Chorus.*

5.

Behind de barn, down on my knees,
  Sing "Polly-wolly-doodle," all the day,
I thought I heard a chicken sneeze,
  Sing "Polly-wolly-doodle," all the day. *Chorus.*

6.

He sneezed so hard wid de hoopin'-cough,
  Sing "Polly-wolly-doodle," all the day,
He sneezed his head an' his tail right off.
  Sing "Polly-wolly-doodle," all the day. *Chorus.*

CAMPTOWN RACES.

Music by Stephen C. Foster.

SOLO.

Gwine to run all night! Gwine to run all day! I'll

bet my mo-ney on de bob-tail nag. Some-bo-dy bet on de bay.

CHORUS.

Gwine to run all night! Gwine to run all day! I'll

bet my mo-ney on de bob-tail nag. Some-bo-dy bet on de bay.

KEMO KIMO.

FULL CHORUS.

Ke - mo, Ki - mo! Dar! oh, whar'? Wid my hi, my ho, and in come Sal - ly, sing-ing,

Some-times pen-ny win-kle, ling-tum, nip-cat. Sing song, Kit-ty, can't you ki'-me, oh!

2.

Milk in de dairy nine days old,
    Sing song, Kitty, can't you ki'-me, oh!
Frogs and de skeeters getting mighty bold,
    Sing song, etc.
Dey try for to sleep, but it ain't no use,
    Sing song, etc.
Deir legs hung out for de chickens to roost,
    Sing song, Kitty, can't you ki'-me, oh! *Full Chorus.*

3.

Dar was a Frog liv'd in a pool,
    Sing song, etc.
Sure he was de biggest fool,
    Sing song, etc.
For he could dance, and he could sing,
    Sing song, etc.
And make de woods around him ring,
    Sing song, Kitty, can't you ki'-me, oh! *Full Chorus.*

ELLIE RHEE.

Words and Music by Sep. Winner.

1. Sweet El - lie Rhee, so dear to me, Is lost for ev - er - more; Our
2. Oh why did I from day to day, Keep wish - ing to be free, And
3. Dey said dat I would soon be free And hap - py all de day, But
4. De war is o - ver now at last, De co - lour'd race is free; Dat

home was down in Ten - nes - see Be - fore dis cru - el war.
from my mas - sa run a - way, And leave my El - lie Rhee?
if dey take me back a - gain I'll neb - ber run a - way.
good time com - in' on so fast I'se wait - ing for to see.
Den

car - ry me back to Ten - nes - see, Back where I long to be, A -

mong de fields of yel - low corn; To my dar - ling El - lie Rhee.

CARMEN DE LALAGES AGNA.

Words by J. D. Symon.   Air – "Ellie Rhee."

(Canit "pastor" quidam solus.)

I.

Heus, fratres, ecce Lalage
Aurora pulchrior!
Et ejus agna parvula
Nive candidior!

    Then carry me back to Old Tennessee,
    There let me live and die,
    Among the fields of yellow, yellow corn,
    When the bloom is on the rye.

2.

Quocunque venit Lalage
Dulcissima; eo
Fidelis agna sequitur
Illam perpetuo. *Chorus.*

3.

Quondam secuta dominam
Audebat progredi
Ad praeceptricis limina
Riserunt pueri. *Chorus.*

4.

Praeceptrix agnam expulit,
Sed prato viridi
Haec expectavit Lalagen
Cum ludo salubri. *Chorus.*

5.

"Quam ob rem", clamant pueri,
"Agna tantopere
Illam amat, praeceptrix, dic
Nobis maturrime?" *Chorus.*

6.

Ad quos serena domina
Ridens suavissime,
"O, agnam amat Lalage",
Respondit tranquille.

    Then carry me back to Old Tennessee,
    There let me live and die,
    Among the fields of yellow, yellow corn,
    When the bloom is on the rye.

SO EARLY IN THE MORNING.

Moderato.

Arr. by J. K. L.

mf

Fine.

1. South Ca - ro - li - na's a sul - try clime, Where we used to work in the
2. When I was young I used to wait, On mas - sa's ta - ble
3. Now mas - sa's dead and gone to rest, Of all de mas - sas

p

sum - mer - time, Mas - sa neath de shade would lay, While we poor nig - gers
lay de plate, Pass de bot - tle when him dry, Brush a - way de
he war best; I neb - ber see de like since I was born, Miss him now he's

toil'd all day.
blue - tail'd fly. So ear - ly in de morn - ing, So ear - ly in de
dead and gone.

p

cres.

GOOD-NIGHT.

2.

Farewell, ladies; farewell, ladies;
Farewell, ladies; we're going to leave you now.
    Merrily, etc.

3.

Sweet dreams, ladies; sweet dreams, ladies;
Sweet dreams, ladies; we're going to leave you now.
    Merrily, etc.

FOR AULD LANG SYNE.

"We'll tak' a cup o' kindness yet."

AULD LANG SYNE.

Either.—
Verse 1. Solo or Tutti 2nd Tenor.
Verse 2. „   „   „   1st Bass.
Verse 3. „   „   „   1st Tenor.
Verse 4. „   „   „   2nd Bass.
Verse 5. Tutti in Unison.
Or, the whole in Chorus.

Arr. by Sir Herbert Oakeley, Mus. Doc., etc.

1. Should auld ac - quain - tance be for - got, And
2. We twa ha'e run a - bout the braes, And
3. We twa ha'e pai - delt i' the burn Frae
4. And here's a hand, my trust - y fière, And
5. And sure - ly ye'll be your pint - stoup, And

nev - er brought to min'? Should auld ac - quain - tance
pu'd the gow - ans fine; But we've wan - der'd mony a
morn - in' sun till dine; But seas be - tween us
gie's a hand o' thine, And we'll tak' a richt guid
sure - ly I'll be mine, And we'll tak' a cup o'

*) From "Eighteen Scottish Melodies arranged for Male Chorus for the Universities of Scotland," and orchestrated for Edinburgh University Musical Society, by Sir Herbert Oakeley. Printed by his kind permission.

BREAD AND BUTTER.

Words by J. S. Clouston.

Music by Robert A. Christison. (1897.)

Soft hearts, pray still your flut - ter; Bright eyes, re -

press those tears; ———— Our quest is bread and

but - ter, So fare - well to you, dears. ————

CHORUS.
Tempo di Valse.

Bread and but-ter, bread and but-ter, Since the Var-si-

cres.

ty be - gan, Cram-ming his head To but-ter his bread

Has been the lot of man. _____ 1. *Repeat Chorus.* 2. man. _____

2.

You've cheered our days between you,
　Your fair selves best know how;
To quite forget we've seen you
　Must be our effort now. *Chorus.*

3.

Good friends, who've stood beside us
　Through many a merry day,
We'll e'en have to divide us,
　And each pursue his way. *Chorus.*

4.

Our company must scatter,
　Our road together ends;
A laughing, crying matter
　It is to part from friends. *Chorus.*

5.

Up with our students' shutter!
　Down with the jovial sign!
We're off for bread and butter,
　Good-bye, stout comrades mine. *Chorus.*

WANDERLIED.

Translation from the German of Justinus Kerner
by F. W. Farrar.*

"Wohlauf noch getrunken."

Allegretto.

1. Ho! drain the bright wine-cup, ho! drink with good cheer, For the hour of our part-ing, my loved ones, is near; Fare-well to the moun-tains, fare-well to my home; My heart in the far world is yearn-ing to roam! Fare-well to the moun-tains, fare-well to my home, My heart in the far world is yearning to roam, yearn-ing to roam.

2. Not long doth the sun in his blue tent re-main, He flames o'er the o-cean, he rolls o'er the plain; The sea-wave grows wea-ry of kiss-ing the shore, And the blasts of the tem-pest, how loud-ly they roar, The sea-wave grows wea-ry of kiss-ing the shore; And the blasts of the tem-pest, how loud-ly they roar, yes, loud-ly roar.

* By kind permission of the Very Rev. Dean Farrar.

CHORUS.

Ju - vi - val - le - ra, Ju - vi - val - le - ra, Ju - vi - val - le - ra - le - ra - le -

ra, Ju - vi - val - le - ra, Ju - vi - val - le - ra, Ju - vi - val - le - ra - le - ra - le - ra.

3.

The bird on the swift cloud is hurried along,
Afar doth it warble its home-loving song;
So speeds the boy-wanderer through forest and fell,
Since his mother earth hasteth, he hasteth as well! Hasteth as well! *Chorus.*

4.

Far away the birds greet him with songs from the blue,
From plains of his home o'er the waters they flew;
And the flowers still around him deliciously bloom,
From his home the soft breezes have borne their perfume, borne their perfume. *Chorus.*

5.

O'er the roofs of his fathers the bird's wing hath flown,
For the wreath of his darling those blossoms were sown,
And love is his guard, and his comrade is love,
So his home will be near him, wherever he rove, where'er he rove. *Chorus.*

AE FOND KISS.

Old Highland Melody.
Arr. by W. Augustus Barratt.

Words by Robert Burns, (1791.)

Slowly, and with tenderness.

1. Ae fond kiss, and then we sev-er! Ae fare-weel, a-las! for ev-er! Deep in heart-wrung tears I'll pledge thee, War-ring sighs and groans I'll wage thee.

2.
Who shall say that Fortune grieves him,
While the star of hope she leaves him?
Me, nae cheerfu' twinkle lights me,
Dark despair around benights me.

3.
I'll ne'er blame my partial fancy:
Naething could resist my Nancy!
But to see her was to love her,
Love but her, and love for ever.

4.
Had we never lov'd sae kindly,
Had we never lov'd sae blindly,
Never met – or never parted,
We had ne'er been broken-hearted.

5.
Fare thee weel, thou first and fairest!
Fare thee weel, thou best and dearest!
Thine be ilka joy and treasure,
Peace, Enjoyment, Love, and Pleasure!

6.
Ae fond kiss, and then we sever!
Ae fareweel, alas, for ever!
Deep in heart-wrung tears I'll pledge thee,
Warring sighs and groans I'll wage thee.

WILL YE NO COME BACK AGAIN?

Words by the Baroness Nairne. (1766 - 1845.)

Air attrib. to Neil Gow, jun. (1795 - 1823.)
Arr. by W. Augustus Barratt.

1. Bon - nie Char - lie's noo a - wa, Safe - ly o'er the friend - ly main;
2. Ye trust - ed in your Hie-land men, They trust-ed you, dear Char - lie!
3. Eng - lish bribes were a' in vain, Tho' puir and puir-er we maun be;

For first verse only.

Mo - ny a heart will break in twa, Should he ne'er come back a - gain.
They kent your hid - ing in the glen, Death and ex - ile brav - ing.
Sil - ler can - na buy the heart That aye beats warm for thine and thee.

CHORUS.

Will ye no come back a - gain? Will ye no come back a - gain?

Bet-ter lo'ed ye can-na be. Will ye no come back a - gain?

4.
We watched thee in the gloamin' hour,
We watched thee in the mornin' grey;
Though thirty thousand pounds they gi'e,
Oh, there is nane that wad betray! *Chorus.*

5.
Sweet's the laverock's note, and lang,
Liltin' wildly up the glen;
But aye to me he sings ae sang,
"Will ye no come back again?" *Chorus.*

The chorus of this song is generally sung by Scots students in speeding a departing guest.

AMICI.

Air, "Annie Lisle."
Arr. by J. K. L.

Andante con moto.

mf

p

1. Our strong band can ne'er be bro-ken, It can nev-er die;
2. Col-lege life is swift-ly pass-ing, Soon its sands are run, But

Far sur-pass-ing wealth un-spo-ken, Seal'd by friend-ship's tie.
while we live we'll ev-er cher-ish Friend-ships here be-gun.

CHORUS. *

A-mi-ci, us-que ad a-ras, Deep grav-en on each heart,

mf *rall.*

Shall be found un - wav-'ring, true, When we from life shall part.

* Sung without accompaniment.

Songs of the Universities.

Vivat Academia!
Vivant professores!
Vivat membrum quodlibet!
Vivant membra quaelibet!
Semper sint in flore!

ST. ANDREWS UNIVERSITY.
CARMEN SECULARE.

Words by
Rev. Lewis Campbell, M.A., LL.D.,
Em. Prof., Univ. St. Andr.

Music by
Sir Herbert Oakeley, LL.D., Mus. Doc.,
Em. Prof., Univ. Edinb.

* The original key, a semitone higher, is preferable.
Printed by permission of the St. Andrews University Musical Society. (The song is orchestrated for that Society by Sir Herbert Oakeley.)

(Verse 5 for special use at University Musical Society's Annual Concerts.)

Al unisono ed assai ritmico.

TENORS and BASSES 8va lower.

ACCOMP.

sempre stacc. il basso

3. Cu - ra fu - it ut sa - git - tam Ar - cu rec - té
5. Mul - tas et so - ci - e - ta'- tes Cœ - tus nos - ter

ten - de-rem: Est ut pi - lam sci - té mit - tam Can - di-dam - que
por - ri-git, Sa - cer E - din - bur - gi va - tes** (Cui sint ho - di -

va - tes vit - tam Fron - te pu - ro ges - ti-tem, Pe - de fol - lem
e - que gra - tes) Mu - si - cam nunc di - ri-git, Al - te - ra gym -

pro - vol-ven-tem, Pen - nâ char-tas il - li-nen-tem, Con - to ma-chi-
nas - ti - ca, Ter - tia his-tri - o - ni-ca, Quar - ta phil-o-

marcato ff e ritardando   *D.C. for Verse 4.*

nam mo-ven - tem Cer - nas nos - trum mi - li - tem.
soph - i - ca, Sur - sum men - tes e - ri-git.

After verse 5 repeat verse 1.

* The lowest note of the right hand chords, if causing any difficulty to an accompanist, may be omitted.

** In allusion to Sir Herbert Oakeley's presence, as Honorary President and Conductor, at the University Musical Society's Annual Concert.

THE PROFS' SONG.

Air founded on "The Dutch Company."

I. Here's to the Rec-tor come to see The stu-dents of this 'Var-si-ty; Head o'er all the Profs and we, The might-iest he in the 'Var-si-ty. With a kai, ai, ai, ai, ah! With a kai, ai, ai, ai, ah! With a kai, ai, ai, ai, ai, ai, ai, ai, ah!

2.

Here's to the Don of the 'Varsity,
The man who's up in the Greek idee,
Which idee, alas for me!
Must be ground for my degree. *Chorus.*

3.

Here's to the Prof. of Humanity,
Likewise the Prof. of Philology;
Latin to he is a mystery,
Without the aid of an English Key. *Chorus.*

4.

Here's to the Prof. of Geometry,
The latest expounder of a, b, c;
But oh! that he and his a + b
Were sunk in the sea of nonentity! *Chorus.*

5.

Here's to the Prof. of Philosophy,
The mystic sage of the 'Varsity,
The man of darkness — the man at sea
In the maze of Responsibility. *Chorus.*

6.

Here's to the Prof. who has come to we,
To cram us in Psychology;
Rare boy he, and rare boys we,
The best in all the 'Varsity! *Chorus.*

7.

Here's to the Prof. of Physiology,
Famous for his jocularity;
Listen to he when he tells a story,
But don't trust its credibility. *Chorus.*

8.

Here's to a Prof. of Divinity,
A man of wondrous ubiquity;
Where'er you be you're sure to see
This man of curiosity. *Chorus*

A SONG OF CENTURIES.
(CARMEN SECULARE.)

Words by Prof. Lewis Campbell.   Air—"Carmen Seculare."

1.

Lo, St. Andrews' Youths before ye,
  Splendid in the scarlet gown,
Whom their Kate, renowned in story,
Sound and whole through years of glory,
  Calls to College from the town.
Manhood from our fathers' merit,
Health from Scotia's air we inherit,
Still with staunch fraternal spirit
  Preachers seek our lives to crown.

2.

Grey professors, learned sages,
  With endurance gifted well,
Lead us onward through the ages,
Labouring o'er the storied pages
  Wisdom gilds with gentle spell.
Logic love we to palaver,
Mathematics much we favour,
Eke a smack we have or savour
  Of what science hath to tell.

3.

Once I cared to point so featly
  Arrows from the bended bow;
Now I *putt* the golf-ball neatly,
Or the poet's garland sweetly
  Busk on my unwrinkled brow.
By the football lightly bounding,
By the sonnet fairly sounding,
By the cannon we're surrounding
  Our battalion you may know.

4.

Few my ranks when all are cited;
  Few than many goodlier are;
Fewer strands in one united,
On the rope-walk firmly plighted,
  Make a stronger cord by far,
Than the crowd that, each his tiny
Bark upon the ocean briny
Paddles, while with rash design he
  Braves the roaring tempest's war.

5.

Lo, St. Andrews' Youths before ye,
  Splendid in the scarlet gown,
Whom their Kate, renowned in story,
Sound and whole through years of glory,
  Calls to College from the town.
Manhood from our fathers' merit,
Health from Scotia's air we inherit,
Still with staunch fraternal spirit
  Preachers seek our lives to crown.

NB. This paraphrase of "Carmen Seculare" is placed on this page instead of the preceding one where properly it should be, in order that the singer who uses the English words, may have them before him, by holding the preceding leaf open, while the accompanist plays the music on page 328.

THE COUNTRY PARSON'S LAMENT.

Words by H. M. B. Reid.

1. Give me back my gown and trencher That were once so dear to me; Better is that life Bo-hemian Than re-spec-ta-bi-li-ty. Oh! This black coat chafes me sad-ly, Ro-man col-lars scrape my chin, And 'tis hard to get i-de-as Out, when there is nothing in.

2.

Give me back my cosy "diggings,"
And its cupboard stored with beer;
Where so oft the merry circle
Filled the air with laugh and cheer.
O those days of thoughtless pleasure_
O those nights of lengthened chat;
Nothing in this lonely mill-round
Can refresh my heart like that!

3.

Jack with laugh that stirred up laughter_
Jim a favourite with the fair_
Mac who nightly slew "Ta Phairshon"_
Joe with philosophic air:
All are now in country manses_
Hebrew vexes them no more;
But the fattest living never
Can bring back those days of yore.

HORAE ANDREANAE.

Words by Dr. George Park.

Air – "Wohlauf noch getrunken."
(See page 322.)

1

Let the wine mantle high to a toast,
  Your ardent souls with rapture greet;
St. Andrews is the theme that I boast,
  No other name to you all can be so sweet.
To thee then, dear 'Varsity, our joyful thoughts
    shall turn;
For thee yet, St. Andrews, untired our passions
    yearn;
For thee alone, thou fairest scene, our hearts this
    night shall glow,
And to thy glorious memories our festive gob-
    lets flow,
      Yes, they shall flow.
  Chorus. Tra la, la.

2

What though we are far from thy shore,
  And many years betwixt have passed away,
Affection brings us nearer than before,
  And memory makes us students yesterday;
We all, *Alma mater,* are thy alumni true,
And all delight with one accord to pay thee
    homage due;
We all are linked for aye with thee in one har-
    monious chain,
And in thy name our common voice appraises
    this refrain,
      This great refrain.
  Chorus. Tra la, la.

3

How happy as Bejants were we,
  Our dress academic as our taste;
Our gowns were red and beautiful to see,
  And we were fond of getting "on the waste."
How oft in full convention we gathered at the
    "Cross,"
And in a gay contention the merry jest would toss;
Our yellow beaks the chorus swelled, the outer
    air to greet,
And vocal breezes wafted it along the classic
    street,
      The classic street.
  Chorus. Tra la, la.

4

What attractions has St. Andrews in its maids!
  Souls of sentiment and miracles of grace,
We have loved, alas! and lost them, but our heads
  Were ne'er so turned in any other place.
On Sunday afternoons among the hillocks we
    would stand,
And watch the taper ankles speeding o'er the
    western sand,
Their silken locks aflying as they struggled in
    the wind,
And they knew not we were dying to follow up
    behind,
      Yes, just behind.
  Chorus. Tra la, la.

5

On the links we drove the matutinal ball,
  With a never-tiring vigour, far afield;
In the matches 'twixt "the College" and "the Hall,"
  It was right seldom either side would yield.
And when the vesper bell had bid us in some
    "bunk" collect,
"Napoleonic" mystery enshrouded the select;
The glowing fire would pale before our humour's
    frequent flash,
And I. O. U's would pass around as frequently
    as cash,
      The same as cash.
  Chorus. Tra la, la.

6.

Then let us shout once more, "St. Andrews, hail!"
  May thy future be as fruitful as thy past!
For thee we'll strive, and sure we'll never fail,
  To make each year a richer than the last.
So long as we can draw a breath we'll sing thy
    lofty fame,
So long as we can drain a cup we'll do it in thy
    name;
Our watchword is thy honour, our dear old 'Varsity,
We'll hand thy name untarnished to remote
    posterity,
      Posterity.
  Chorus. Tra la, la.

THE PROBATIONER'S FAREWELL TO ST. ANDREWS.

Words by H. M. B. Reid.

Tune —"Hunting the Hare."

Arr. by J. K. L.

1. The last words of part-ing have dropp'd from my lips, The
last pipe of friend-ship has van-ish'd in va-pour; I've paid all my bills and
got the re-ceipts From land-la-dy, gro-cer, to-bac-co-nist, dra-per;
The 'bus-horse is jang-ling his bri-dle with-out— A-las! I must leave thee, St.

2.

How often the sea-breeze has blown o'er my face,
    As I walked o'er the links in the bright summer air,
And love hung all trembling on sweet maiden lips,
    And little I recked of trouble or care!
But now all is ended: the turmoil of life
    From love-wildered musings my pathway must sever;
Yet still while I wander in search of a kirk,
    St. Andrews, thy memory leaveth me never!

3.

Farewell! the shrill whistle is blowing the start,
    Farewell! ancient streets that must know me no more;
Perhaps some kind heart may remember me there—
    Some heart that has throbb'd for me often before.
Farewell, dearest comrades in work and in play—
    I leave you behind me, it may be for ever;
But still while I wander in search of a kirk,
    St. Andrews, thy memory leaveth me never!

ABERDEEN UNIVERSITY.

CANTICUM IN ALMAM MATREM
Abredonensem.

Latin words by Principal Sir William D. Geddes, LL.D.
English words by John Malcolm Bulloch, M.A.

Set to Music for Men's Voices
by John Kirby.

er - go summ(o)ho - no - re Al - mam ma - trem con - ci - na - mus.

2.

Salve, prisca Toga Rubra,
Rubra Toga, Toga Rubra,
   Aulæ vestis Regiæ;
Mox per scholas et delubra
Scotiam vox sonet supra_
Pereat vetus colubra
   Sordis ignorantiæ. *Chorus.*

3.

Proinde nobilis Capella,
Ædium nostrarum stella,
   Cœlitus renideat:
Sic exundent sacra cella
Nectaris sapore mella,
Nec Dis ater atra fella
   Immiscere audeat. *Chorus.*

4.

Vosque proles Mariscalli,
Advocati, Medicelli,
   Protegant vos numina;
Seu peritia scalpelli,
Seu juridici duelli,
Semper nescii refelli,
   Fulgeatis lumina. *Chorus.*

5.

Salve tota gens togata,
Pervicax sed cauta cata,
   Matris Academiæ,
Per Parnassi ludens prata
Gloriose, neve fata
Lædant unquam læta sata
   Almæ Academiæ. *Chorus.*

6.

Quare sempiterno flore
Stet perennis in honore,
   Mater Academia,
Palladis pollens amore,
Cynthiæ nitens sub rore,
Cynthii splendens decore,
   Mater Academia. *Chorus.*

2.

Hail, the Gownsman's ancient scarlet!
Scarlet toga, toga scarlet,
   King's attire of motherhood.
Yet through Scotland's schools afar, let
All thy light like blazing starlet
Pierce the gloom, and lead the varlet
   Into wisdom's brotherhood. *Chorus.*

3.

May our noble Chapel, gleaming
Orb of all our founder's scheming,
   Be of Heaven prophetical;
While the fane with honey teeming
Sends its fragrant nectar streaming;
While no evil fate blaspheming
   Taints with creed heretical. *Chorus*

4.

Marischal, younger Alma Mater,
Law and Medicine founded later,
   Gods give all security;
Whether as the surgeon greater,
Or forensical debater,
Ever failure's steadfast hater,
   Light the world's obscurity. *Chorus.*

5.

Life to students, oft audacious,
Yet in wisdom's ways sagacious,
   Spite of all perversity!
In Parnassus' meads vivacious,
Children, may thy lot be gracious!
Save from every fate rapacious
   This, your University. *Chorus.*

6.

May thy glory know no failing,
Greater heights of honour scaling,
   Mater Academia.
In Minerva's love prevailing,
On Diana's dew regaling,
Great Apollo's bays entailing,
   Mater Academia. *Chorus.*

SALVE BOREALE LUMEN!

Carmen Abredonense.

HAIL THE NORTHERN BEACON.

Condidit
Prof. Johannes Wight Duff, A. M.

Musicis modis accommodavit
Carolus Sanford Terry, A. M.

"Salve Boreale Lumen," originally written by Professor Wight Duff as a College song for Newcastle-on-Tyne, was re-written by its author to suit the most northerly University in Scotland.

SALVE BOREALE LUMEN.

Carmen Abredonense.

HAIL THE NORTHERN BEACON.

1.

Unisoni

Salve boreale lumen
Resplendentis Scotiæ!
Salve venerandum numen
Urbis Abredoniæ!
Alma Mater, ave! salve!
Floreas in sæcula!

I.

Hail the Northern Beacon, guiding
Scottish students with its ray!
Hail the sanctity presiding
O'er the Granite City grey!
Alma Mater! welfare, wisdom
Grace thee to eternity!

2.

Divisi

Binos amnes, Devam, Donam,
Una voce canite:
Ibi Turrim, hic Coronam
Laudibus extollite.
Alma Mater, etc.

2.

"Dee and Don!" in blended praises
Tuneful through our pæan rings:
"Dee and Don!" to memory raises
Marischal Tower and Crown of King's.
Alma Mater! etc.

3.

Viri

Tomostineis tradentes
Jubilate cantico:

Feminæ

Togam rubram exuentes
Indulgete gaudio.

Omnes

Alma Mater, etc.

3.

Bookworms all our books may borrow;
We will sing our merry glee:
Doff the red gown till tomorrow;
Harmony shall set us free.
Alma Mater! etc.

4.

Unisoni

Jam concentu gaudeamus
Devanenses filii!
Almam Matrem salutamus:
Astent di propitii!
Alma Mater, etc.

4.

Now in "Bon accord" rejoicing,
Prove Devanha's fealty,
Alma Mater's praises voicing
With a Godsent energy.
Alma Mater! etc.

5.

Divisi

Durat neque scit domari
Scopulorum suboles:
Robore dotetur pari
Et nostrorum indoles!
Alma Mater, etc.

5.

As the granite bids defiance
To the ravages of years,
So be King's and Marischal's scions
Granite-strong in their careers!
Alma Mater! etc.

6.

Feminæ

Academicæ sorores
Concinentes floreant!

Viri

Floreant et professores
Et qui illos audiant!

Omnes

Alma Mater, etc.

6.

Sisters linked by study nearer
Greet we in sincerity:
To Professor and to hearer
Wish we aye prosperity.
Alma Mater! etc.

7.

Divisi

*Vivat quaelibet doctrina_*
Sancta theologia,
Artes, Musae, Medicina,
Cum juris peritia.
Alma Mater, etc.

7.

Long may truth all learning nourish
In the University!
Music, Arts and Medicine flourish,
Science, Law, Divinity!
Alma Mater! etc.

8.

Unisoni

Vivat studiosa proles
Pia reverentia:
Mente moveatur moles:
Floreat scientia!
Alma Mater, etc.

8.

May the sons of Alma Mater
Ever love her loyally!
Mente moles moveatur!
Triumph knowledge royally!
Alma Mater! etc.

THE SUNNIEST SEASON OF LIFE.

Words by John Malcolm Bulloch, M. A.

Music by John Kirby.

Con spirito. ♩ = 76.

1. O where is the sphere like a student career, With its in-fin-i-tes-i-mal trouble, Its hope and its fear with its chances and cheer, Its tri-als that burst as a bubble? Phil-o-sophers say that life is no play, And sometimes they say so with rea-son; Be that as it may, yet the stu-dent's brief day, Is the hap-py-go-luck-i-est sea-son.

CHORUS.

Tenors. (8ve lower.)

Be it spent in the North, By the Clyde, by the Forth, Or yet in the Kingdom of Fife, 'Tis the

Basses.

maddest, most merry, The sad-dest to bu-ry, The sun-niest season of life.

2. What badge of renown can compare with the Gown,
  Our great academical glory;
To be reared by the Crown in the sleepy old town,
  Where all is so silent and hoary?
Imperial King's, what a majesty clings
  To thee from the echoing ages!
The silence takes wings when there merrily rings
  The voice of thy embryo sages.
        Chorus.

3. For scientist fame, so accustomed to claim
  A view of creation impartial,
For those who would aim at the cure of the maim —
  Stand open the portals of Marischal.
Yet the barons of bones, both the dons and the drones;
  Are ever the first to acknowledge
There's less in the stones of the goodliest thrones
  Than what may be found in their college.
        Chorus.

4. The student of Greek with his training to seek
  The joy of historic emotion,
Divines that are meek, and the legalist sleek,
  The med. with his pills and his lotion —
With scarce an alloy to disturb and annoy
  We always are happy and airy.
And now to our joy comes the damozel coy,
  A true undergraduate fairy.
        Chorus.

GLASGOW UNIVERSITY.

MORIAR, MELPOMENE.

Words by W. A. A. Armstrong, M.A.

Music by C. W. Glover.

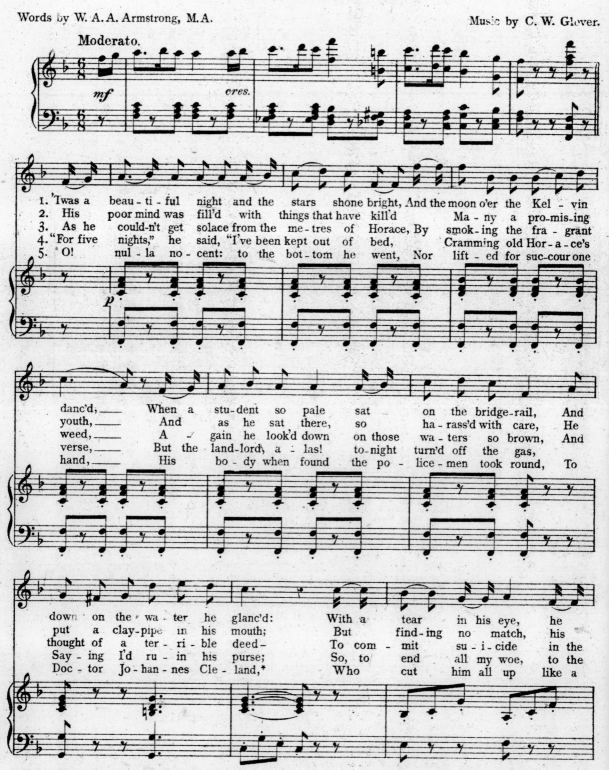

* Note.— This song was written for a Latin Class Supper in 1873. Dr. Allen Thomson being at that time Professor of Anatomy in the University, lines 2 and 4 of verse 5 ran— "*Ut pisces in maribus run;*" "*To Doctor Allenus Thomson.*"

After first four verses go on to the chorus.

For last Verse only, then on to chorus.

Nev-er stu-dy too late, or you'll meet the same fate. Mor-i-ar, Mel-po-me-ne.

CHORUS.

Mor-i-ar,____ Mor-i-ar,____ Mor-i-ar, O! Mel-po-me-ne,____ Mor-i-ar,____ Mor-i-ar,____ Mor-i-ar, O! Mel-po-me-ne.____

EDINBURGH UNIVERSITY.
CHANCELLOR INGLIS.*

Words by Sir Douglas Maclagan.

Air, "Kate Dalrymple".

1. I'm pass'd, I'm pass'd And capp'd at last, I'm qua-li-fied and free now, On pasteboard neat, Or brass doorplate, To write my-self M. B. now. I'm full of joy, With-out al-loy, And my whole frame with plea-sure ting-les, For in gown and in hood, I've been capp'd by the good And ma-gic hand of Chancel-lor Ing-lis!

* The Right Hon. John Inglis, late Lord Justice General, and Chancellor of the University.

CHANCELLOR INGLIS.

1.

I'm pass'd, I'm pass'd
And capp'd at last;
I'm qualified and free now,
  On pasteboard neat,
  Or brass doorplate,
To write myself M. B. now.
  I'm full of joy,
  Without alloy,
And my whole frame with pleasure tingles,
  For in gown and in hood,
  I've been capp'd by the good
And magic hand of Chancellor Inglis!

2.

How proud my mien
When I hear the Dean
Proclaim my name and nation!
  How swells my heart
  When I play my part
In this great graduation!
  For there's one with a pair
  Of blue eyes fair,
Who from the rest my figure singles,
  And feels as if she
  Were a bit of me,
When I am capped by Chancellor Inglis.

3.

How pleasant the tap
  Of the velvet cap,
Which old tratition teaches
  Was made from the rear
  Of a half-used pair
Of George Buchanan's breeches.
  I don't know well
  If in this tale
The mythic with historic mingles
  But the cap is a fact,
  And so is the tact
Of the erudite hand of Chancellor Inglis.

4.

I yet know not
Upon what spot
In practice I may settle,
  Or if folks will see,
  As they should in me,
A man of sterling metal.
  But when the due
  Fees shall accrue,
And the sovereign with the shilling jingles,
  Its pleasant little chime
  Will recall the time
Of the magic touch of Chancellor Inglis.

5.

My future home
May be in some
Of England's rich domains now,
  Or in the North,
  Beyond the Forth,
Among the mountain chains now;
  Or it may by
  The Borders lie,
'Mong Johnstones, Elliots, Scotts and Pringles;
  But wherever it be,
  I'll teach them to see
The worth of a man that was capped by Inglis.

6.

And who shall say,
  But some fine day,
When practice then increases,
  To my door there may come
  A neat little brougham,
And pair with smartish paces:
  And when folks spy
  My nags go by,
Their collars, traces, reins, surcingles,
  They'll say without doubt,
  That's a smart turn-out
Of the man that was capped by Chancellor Inglis.

7.

And when I may,
  On holiday,
Enjoy release from duty,
  With a sweet little wife,
  The charm of my life,
Admiring nature's beauty;
  Then when we roam,
  Away from home,
In sunny fields or bosky dingles,
  We'll both of us know
  That the pleasure we owe
To the magic touch of Chancellor Inglis.

8.

Now long may he
Our Chancellor be;
Now let the glasses clatter
  To his health, and the fame
  Of the ancient dame
That is our Alma Mater;
  And as the Tay
  And mighty Spey
Flow full-streamed over rocks and shingles,
  Let the red wine now
  In rivers flow
To the jolly good health of Chancellor Inglis.

THE TOUNIS COLLEDGE.

Words by Dr. David Rorie.

Air – "Bonnie Dundee."
(See page 44.)

1.

We sing not thy praises in Latin or Greek,
But just in the common old language we speak;
When we sound thy fair fame no such hindrance we brook—
All hail to the Thistle and Castle and Book!
Chorus. Come fill up your bumpers as full as you can,
      And drink to this toast every true-hearted man,
      Be ye living by land, be ye sailing by sea,
      "Love, life, and all honour to Our Varsitee!"

2.

Where thy old buildings stand in a regular square
Poor Darnley went rocket-like up in the air,
And as Kirk o' Field down to her foundations shook
Then sprang up the Thistle and Castle and Book! *Chorus.*

3.

Then Jamie the Sixth in his wisdom decreed
That Scotland of thee had the sorest of need;
Like a wise man all sorts of precautions he took,
Combining the Thistle and Castle and Book! *Chorus.*

4.

Here men of all nations mapped out by man-kind
Acknowledge supremacy only of mind,
And the surgical knife and the Pastoral Crook
Gain glory for Thistle and Castle and Book! *Chorus.*

5.

Could the shades of thy great ones but stand in the quad,
In the forms that they bore ere they went 'neath the sod,
A genius would fill each available nook,
An honour to Thistle and Castle and Book! *Chorus.*

6.

When Macaulay's New Zealander comes to the North,
And, guide-book in hand, views the banks of the Forth,
He will mouth maledictions at Time and his hook
For harming the Thistle and Castle and Book! *Chorus.*

(Thistle, Castle and Book are the arms of Edinburgh University.)

THE BOTANY CLASS.

Words by a Student of 1880.

Air "Chancellor Inglis," *alias* Kate "Dalrymple."

I.

It's a guid mony year
Sin' I cam' here,
An' the time that my tale commences;
When I handed in my name,
An' for a poun' I became
Civ. Univ. Academ. Edinensis.
My prelim. noo was o'er,
E'en for Greek I cared no more,
For I'd proved that I'd had a guid education;
So next I was told,
To be sure to get enrolled,
In accordance wi' the Act o' Registration.

2.

To Inverleith next day
I was early away,
In the beautiful summer weather;
An' I took a front seat,
Where the flowers were so sweet,
Near a big bonnie pot o' heather;
An' I lookit at the wa'
An' the diagrams braw,
But I soon was distractit frae "stamens and pistils,"
By a' the crowd o' boys
Makin' sic a fearfu' noise
Wi' the thumpin' o' their sticks and their whistles.

3.

Then loudly did they cheer
When the Professor did appear,
Wha ken'd a' matters botanic,
An' announced wi' a smile
That he'd occupy a while
In contrasting the "mineral" and "organic."
An' plainly he did show
That a cairngorm couldna grow,
Except by a kind o' a superaddition,
An' couldna generate its kind,
E'en though it had the mind,
For the want o' the powers o' nutrition.

4.

The next thing he did state,
Was that a' things organate,
Into "animals" and "plants" maun be divided;
An' he showed how the one,
Wi' the chlorophyll and sun,
Decomposed what the other had provided;
Then he gave a heap o' rules,
For the use o' learned fools,
"But nane o' them," said he, "is perfect to decide 'em."
Hech! I thocht o' Noah's ark
And the grand old patriarch,
An' I wunnered how he managed to divide 'em.

5.

So ilka morn like a bird,
I flew doon to him and heard
O' pitcher plants and polyanths and umbels,
O' nepenthe's little trap,
O' the circulating sap,
Wi' mony a bonnie flow'r my mem'ry jumbles.
An' oft on Saturday
We turned our work to play,
An' climbed the ben or scoured the moor for species
rare and dainty;
Yet never did he tire
To name the plants we did admire,
Nor cared though there were twa or twenty.

6.

But alas! now he's dead,
His gentle spirit's fled
To the land o' flowers eternal.
Yet I ne'er can forget
His face that haunts me yet,
Nor his manner so kind and paternal.
An' there's nane that knew him weel,
That canna but feel,
Though the Chancellor's cap each head is adorning,
That it's much that we owe,
Of the blessings we know,
To Dickson at eight in the morning.

APPENDICES AND INDEXES.

Bibliography.

THE SCOTTISH STUDENTS' SONG BOOK,

Published for

THE SCOTTISH STUDENTS' SONG BOOK COMMITTEE, LTD.,

London: BAYLEY & FERGUSON, 2 Gt. Marlborough Street, W.
Glasgow: 54 Queen Street.

Large 8vo; issued in paper covers, 3s. net; in cloth, gilt lettering on front and back, 4s. 6d. net; in leather, 6s. 6d. net.

FIRST EDITION: Introduction by Professor Blackie; Editor's Preface; pp. vi. 242. Published 1st April, 1891. Printed from Engraved Plates. No printers' imprint. N.D.

SECOND EDITION: Same as First, but with notes added to several Songs. 3rd July, 1891.

THIRD EDITION: Revised and Enlarged. Introduction by Professor Blackie; Editors' Preface; pp. 274. 1st June, 1892.

FOURTH EDITION: Same as Third, but printed from type at Glasgow University Press. 28th April, 1893.

FIFTH EDITION: Same as the Fourth, with the exception of one Song for which new words were substituted. 30th April, 1896.

SIXTH EDITION: Again Revised and Enlarged; Introduction as above; Editors' Preface; pp. viii. 360. Appendices (12 pp.): Bibliography; Editors' Prefaces to First and Third Editions; Notes about Contributors; Indexes. Paper cover, 3s. net; cloth, 4s. 6d. net. December, 1897.

POCKET EDITION: Cr. 8vo, with voice-parts only of the music printed, in staff and sol-fa notations; pp. 384. 22nd December, 1892.

POCKET EDITION: Cr. 8vo. Tonic Sol-fa pp. 370; Cloth, 2s. Words only, Pott 8vo., pp. 294; Limp cloth, 9d.

POCKET EDITION: Tonic Sol-fa Notation 372 pp., Impl. 16mo., September, 1898.

POCKET EDITION: Words only, 296 pp., Pott. 8vo., November, 1898.

Editors' Preface to First Edition.

THE want of a Collection of Songs for the use of students has long been felt in Scotland, but hitherto no attempt has been made to meet it. Some four or five years ago, indeed, a Committee was appointed at St. Andrews to collect and publish the songs in vogue among the students of that University; but the difficulties of such an enterprise were so many and so great that it was ultimately agreed to abandon the scheme and to recommend the preparation of an Inter-University Song-Book under the auspices of the four Scottish Students' Representative Councils.

In December, 1889, such a recommendation was made by the President of the St. Andrews Council to the representatives of the four Councils assembled in conference at Glasgow; and as a result, the Committee was appointed which is responsible for the production of this volume.

The aim of the Editors has been to adapt the Collection as much as possible to what they conceive to be the wants of students; and if they have not been altogether successful in attaining this end, they trust that the difficulties under which they have laboured may be a sufficient excuse. One of the difficulties students will be ready to appreciate—that the whole of the work in connection with the preparation of the book and its passage through the press has been carried out in the midst of the heavy demands of college and professional work. It should also be remembered that not one of the Scottish Universities, except St. Andrews, has ever possessed anything like a body of Students' Songs, and that therefore the present edition is to a great extent an experiment which can be improved only after it has been thoroughly tried by use.

In sending out this volume, the Editors must record their deep indebtedness to all who have in any way assisted in the production of it. Their thanks are specially due to Sir HERBERT OAKELEY for the generous liberality with which he placed his compositions and arrangements at their disposal; and to Professor BLACKIE for his great interest in the work, and for his valuable assistance and liberal contributions. They are also indebted, among many others, to Dr. A. C. MACKENZIE. Sir DOUGLAS MACLAGAN, Canon FARRAR, Mr. JOHN ADDINGTON SYMONDS, Dr. JOHN SMITH, Dr. J. D. GILLESPIE, etc. Nor must they omit to acknowledge their great obligations to the publishers of the book, but for whose ever-ready assistance and indefatigable care, their labour and difficulties would have been vastly increased.

Finally, they desire to acknowledge their obligations to the following firms for permission to reprint certain copyright songs: Messrs. CHAPPELL & CO., Messrs. HOPWOOD & CREW, EDWIN ASHDOWN, Limited, Messrs. NOVELLO, EWER & CO., Messrs. E. KÖHLER & SON; and especially to Messrs. I. SUCKLING & CO., of Toronto, and Messrs. CHAPPELL & CO., for permission to reproduce twenty-three songs and arrangements from "The Toronto University Song Book."

If in respect to any song there has been unintentional infringement of copyright, the Editors have to express their regret for an error they were anxious to avoid; and they trust that any mistake of this kind will be forgiven.

As much of the music in this book is printed with voice-parts only, it should be noted that in many cases the upper stave should be played an octave lower than it is written.

March, 1891.

MILLAR PATRICK, M.A., St. Andrews, *Convener*.
WILLIAM NELSON, Glasgow.
J. MALCOLM BULLOCH, M.A., Aberdeen.
A. STODART WALKER, Edinburgh.

Note by the St. Andrews Editor.

I THINK it right to state, in explanation of the smallness of the St. Andrews section of the Collegiate songs, that whenever a St. Andrews song contained nothing to indicate a special connection with that University, I included it in the Miscellaneous collection as suitable for general use. "The Bejant's Song" and one or two others of less importance have been excluded on account of difficulties as to the copyright of the music; and the "Carmen seculare Andreanopolitanorum" has not been included, because the St. Andrews University Musical Society (proprietors of the copyright) refuse the necessary permission.

M. P.

Preface to Third Edition.

IN issuing this new and revised edition of "The Scottish Students' Song Book," the Editors desire to acknowledge the kindly reception accorded to the first.

Owing to various difficulties, the former edition was unsatisfactory in many ways: and the first opportunity was taken of carrying out extensive improvements. Several numbers that appeared in the first edition have been omitted in this; but more than sufficient compensation has been made by the introduction of a large number of entirely new songs, which, it is hoped, will add to the popularity and the value of the collection. The chief improvement, however, is in the music, all of which has been revised with the utmost care. For this important work the Editors were fortunate in securing the services of Mr. W. HENRY MAXFIELD, Mus. Bac., F.C.O., of whose painstaking and sympathetic work they gladly offer the most cordial acknowledgment. Rearrangements have been made wherever necessary or desirable, effort being made in all cases to combine simplicity with effectiveness. Special care has been taken to place all the songs within the range of male voices. In most cases the choruses are arranged for four parts—two Tenors, Baritone, and Bass; but there are several instances of three-part arrangements, in which the second part may be taken either by a low Tenor or by a Baritone.

It is hoped that the general result may be satisfactory to those for whom the book is immediately intended, and that it may also commend itself to many of the musical public, for whose use the collection is in many ways adapted.

The Editors have again to record their deep indebtedness to all who have assisted them in their work. Their thanks are specially due to Sir HERBERT OAKELEY for the generous liberality with which he placed his compositions and arrangements at their disposal; and to Professor BLACKIE for his great interest in the work, and for his valuable assistance and liberal contributions. They are also indebted, among many others, to Dr. A. C. MACKENZIE, Sir DOUGLAS MACLAGAN, Archdeacon FARRAR, Mr. JOHN ADDINGTON SYMONDS, Dr. JOHN SMITH, the Rev. H. M. B. REID, B.D., etc. Nor must they omit to acknowledge their great obligations to the publishers of the book, but for whose ever-ready assistance and indefatigable care their labour and difficulties would have been vastly increased.

Finally, they desire to acknowledge their obligations to the following firms, for permission to reprint certain copyright songs: Messrs. BLACKWOOD and Messrs. MACLEHOSE; Messrs. CHAPPELL & CO.; Messrs. HOPWOOD & CREW; EDWIN ASHDOWN, Limited; Messrs. NOVELLO, EWER & Co.; Messrs. E. KÖHLER & SON; Mr. JOHN BLOCKLEY; and especially to Messrs. I. SUCKLING & CO., of Toronto, and Messrs. CHAPPELL & CO., for permission to reproduce a number of copyright songs and arrangements from "The Toronto University Song Book."

If in respect to any song there has been unintentional infringement of copyright, the Editors have to express their regret for an error they were anxious to avoid; and they trust that any mistake of this kind will be forgiven.

May, 1892.

Notes about some Contributors.

" Then shall our names . . .
Be in their flowing cups freshly remembered."—HENRY V. iv. 13.

AYTOUN, WILLIAM EDMONDSTOUNE (1813-65), Professor of Rhetoric and Belles-Lettres in Edinburgh University, 1845 ; was one of the most brilliant members of the North and Blackwood literary *coterie*, and in his critical work especially showed all the strength and all the faults of that school. Author of *Firmilian, a Spasmodic Tragedy*, a satire on the " Spasmodic School," then at the height of its vogue (1854); *Lays of the Scottish Cavaliers ; Bothwell*, a narrative poem, etc. ; joint author, with Sir Theodore Martin, of *The Bon Gaultier Ballads*, from which the famous " Massacre of Macpherson " (Ta Fhairshon) is taken (p. 246).

BARING-GOULD, REV. SABINE (b. 1834), educated at Clare College, Cambridge (M.A.), now squire and rector of Lew Trenchard, Devon ; a writer of almost unbounded versatility ; began his literary work in the field of mediæval research, publishing various works on *Myths of the Middle Ages* and similar subjects ; has written since numerous contributions to theological literature, notably his *Origin and Development of Religious Belief*, and his *Lives of the Saints ;* of late years has become most widely known as the author of *Mehalah* and many other powerful works of fiction ; and, within a more limited circle, has become known as an indefatigable enthusiast, and probably the first living authority, on the subject of English folk-songs ; has published *A Garland of Country Song*, and *Songs of the West*, and edited an extensive collection of *English Minstrelsie*. Mr. Baring-Gould, who re-wrote and modernised " When Joan's ale was new " (p. 178), informs us that " There is a tavern in the town " is an American adaptation of a Cornish folk-song, " The brisk young miner," and that the air of " The wearing of the green " is not Irish, but English.

BARRATT, W. AUGUSTUS (b. 1874), a rising young composer, in 1893 won a scholarship for composition, open to Great Britain ; has published *Sir Patrick Spens*, a ballad ; *The Death of Cuthullin*, a cantata, of which he also wrote the libretto ; *Kemp Owyne*, a ballad-overture for orchestra ; *Lancelot and Elaine*, a cantata, in collaboration

with Mr. J. St. A. Johnson ; and some forty songs (pp. 11, 14, etc.).

BERRY, RICHARD JAMES ARTHUR, M.D., F.R.C.S. (Edin.), a Lecturer in Anatomy in the Edinburgh Extra-mural School ; late President of the Royal Medical Society, etc. ; translator of a work of Talamon ; a frequent contributor to the scientific journals, and, chiefly of verse, to the University magazines (pp. 19, 28).

BLACKIE, JOHN STUART (1809-1895), Professor of Humanity in Marischal College, Aberdeen, 1841-52 ; Professor of Greek in the University of Edinburgh, 1852-82 ; founder of the Chair of Celtic in the University of Edinburgh. Principal works : *Homer and the Iliad, The Wise Men of Greece, The Tragedies of Æschylus* in English verse, *Self-Culture, Four Phases of Morals, The Wisdom of Goethe, Songs of Religion and Life, Songs of the Highlands and Islands, Messis Vitæ*, a *Life of Burns*, etc., etc. An enthusiastic lover of music, Professor Blackie published a collection of *The War Songs of the Germans*, and, in 1869, a small volume of " Songs for Students and University Men," under the title *Musa Burschicosa*. He hailed with great delight the proposal to issue this book, placed all his songs at the editors' disposal, and by writing the introduction, and otherwise, did much to aid the enterprise and to ensure its success.

BRODIE-INNES, J. W., LL.B., Edinburgh, a member of the Faculty of Advocates and of the English Bar (p. 144).

BULLOCH, JOHN MALCOLM, M.A., the Aberdeen representative on the Committee of Editors of this book, was for some years on the staff of *The Aberdeen Free Press*, and is now sub-editor of *The Sketch ;* was for many years the leading spirit in the editorship of *Alma Mater*, the Aberdeen University Magazine, and is still a contributor to its columns ; is the author of a *History of Aberdeen University*, and has published various books of verse, notably *College Carols* (1894) ; is a frequent contributor to many of the leading London newspapers and magazines.

CAMPBELL, REV. LEWIS, M.A. (Oxon.), LL.D., for many years Professor of Greek in the University of St. Andrews, now Professor Emeritus; editor of the text of *Sophocles* for the Clarendon Press, and author of a translation of the Seven Plays in verse; editor also of Plato's *Theætetus*, etc., for the same press; co-editor, with Jowett, of Plato's *Republic*, etc.; with Dr. Evelyn Abbott, editor of *Jowett's Life and Letters*; author of *The Christian Ideal*, etc. (pp. 328, 331).

CHRISTISON, ROBERT A., eldest son of Sir Alexander Christison, Bart., and grandson of the late Sir Robert Christison, until recently was a captain in the Edinburgh Artillery, at present holds a commission in the British Guiana Mounted Police; has written several songs of high quality. The song on page 320 was written specially for this collection.

CLOUSTON, J. S., Barrister-at-Law, a graduate of Oxford, has been a frequent contributor to various University Magazines, and has recently made contributions, chiefly of verse and fiction, to the London press. The words of the song on page 320 originally appeared in a slightly different form in *The Student*, Edinburgh University Magazine.

COBB, GERARD F. (b. 1838), educated at Marlborough College, and at Cambridge, graduated with double first honours; Fellow of Trinity, 1863; president of the University Musical Society for many years, and chairman of the University Board of Musical Studies for fifteen years. Mr. Cobb has published numerous works, as, for example,—Quintet in C, pf. and strings; suite, *Voices of the Sea*, pf.; Prize Madrigal, *Sleeping Beauty*; *Six Songs*, etc.; but is most widely known by his admirable settings of Mr. Rudyard Kipling's *Barrack Room Ballads*, two of which he set specially for this book (pp. 94 and 96).

CRAIGIE, WILLIAM A., M.A., St. Andrews (honours in classics), 1889; B.A., Oriel, Oxford (first-class honours), 1893; studied also in Copenhagen, 1892-93; Assistant Professor of Humanity, St. Andrews, 1893-97; now a member of the staff of the great Oxford English Dictionary. Author of many articles in the *Scottish Review*, *Folk-Lore*, *Proceedings of Society of Antiquaries*, etc.; also of *A Primer of Burns*, and a volume on *Scandinavian Folk Lore* (1897); and co-editor, with Mr. Andrew Lang, of Messrs. Methuen's edition of *The Poems and Songs of Burns*. (See p. 87.)

DAVIDSON, THOMAS, "The Scottish Probationer" (1838-70), a preacher of the United Presbyterian Church. The story of his life, by Dr. James Brown, has become a classic in Scottish biography. His song, *The Yang-tsi-Kiang*, was suggested by a chat, while on one of his journeys as a preacher, with an old woman, who told him that one of her sons was "a soldier far away on the banks of the Yang-tsi-Kiang." It was published in a book of Songs for Children, in Glasgow, in 1869; was one

of the gathering-songs of the supporters of Carlyle in the contest which resulted in the Sage's election to the Lord Rectorship of Edinburgh University, and has been a favourite student-song ever since. The music was written, not as Dr. Brown says, by Davidson himself, but by the lady to whom he was engaged to be married, Alison Hay Dunlop, from whose manuscript the setting on page 106 of this book is taken.

DRINKWATER, DR. T. W., a lecturer on Analytical Chemistry in the Edinburgh Medical School; author of numerous contributions to the discussion of questions of scientific interest, chiefly in the region of Chemistry; and well known in Edinburgh as the author of many popular university and topical songs (p. 176).

DUFF, JOHN WIGHT (b. 1866), Gold Medallist and Dux Aberdeen Grammar School, 1882; graduated at Aberdeen with first-class Classical Honours and as Simpson Greek Prizeman; elected an open scholar of Pembroke College, Oxford, and awarded a first-class in Moderations and in Literæ Humaniores; studied also at the University of Leipzig; for some time Assistant Professor of Greek in Aberdeen, and engaged in literary work; in 1893, appointed Professor of English Literature and Classics in the Durham College of Science, Newcastle-on-Tyne; has since then taken an active part in drafting and organizing the curriculum in letters instituted there by the University of Durham; has acted as a University Extension Lecturer in English Literature, and has several times been examiner for the Degree in Classics and Philosophy (p. 338).

GEDDES, SIR WILLIAM, LL.D., the distinguished Principal of the University of Aberdeen, formerly Professor of Greek for many years (p. 336).

KIPLING, RUDYARD, who was not inaptly called "The Man from Nowhere," when with his *Plain Tales from the Hills*, his stories of the famous *Soldiers Three*, and other Indian stories, he first astonished and delighted the reading world, has now one of the most distinguished and secure literary reputations of our time. Chief works in prose :—*Plain Tales, Soldiers Three, Life's Handicap, Many Inventions, The Light that Failed, The Jungle Books, Captains Courageous*; and in verse : *Departmental Ditties, Barrack-room Ballads*, and *The Seven Seas*. From this last book the two songs on pages 94 and 96 of this book are, with Mr. Kipling's kind permission, reprinted, and published with music for the first time.

MACKENZIE, W. A. (b. 1870), educated at Alness Public School, Tain Royal Academy, and at the Grammar School and Marischal College, Aberdeen; studied medicine for some time, but in 1891 abandoned it for journalism, and now occupies a post on the literary staff of *Black and White*. Mr. Mackenzie says that he "began to rhyme when ten years of age, and—unfortunately, some say—has not yet given up the habit " ; but those who know the one or two small books of verse which he has printed for practically private circulation, and from one of which *Shon Campbell* (p. 11) is taken, will agree in disagreeing with the " some," if they exist at all, and in looking forward with great interest to the issue of his first formally published volume.

MACLAGAN, SIR DOUGLAS, M.D., LL.D., F.R.C.P., etc., Emeritus Professor of Medical Jurisprudence in the University of Edinburgh ; Surgeon-General of the Queen's Bodyguard in Scotland, etc. ; has held the positions of President of the Royal Society of Edinburgh and President of the Royal College of Physicians, Edinburgh ; author of many contributions to the medical journals on materia medica, practice of medicine, and medical jurisprudence ; has written also numerous songs and poems, of which a volume has been published under the title *Nugæ Canoræ Medicæ* (pp. 4 and 344).

MELVILLE, A. P., a Writer to the Signet ; was the first editor of *The Student*, the organ of the Students' Representative Council of the University of Edinburgh ; has published much poetry of high quality and acknowledged beauty, and is the author of a *History of the Union between England and Scotland* (p. 44).

NEAVES, CHARLES (Lord Neaves), formerly one of the Senators of the College of Justice ; author of many essays in verse, for the most part contributed to *Blackwood's Magazine*, from which a number of them were reprinted under the title, *Songs and Verses, Social and Scientific, by an old Contributor to " Maga "* (p. 176).

NELSON, REV. WILLIAM, the Glasgow representative on the Committee of Editors of this book, was trained first for the teaching profession, but after some years spent in it, decided to enter the Church, and after studying at the University and the Free Church College in Glasgow was, in 1892, ordained to the charge of Shettleston Free Church ; acted for some years previously as Choir-master, first in the Free Church, Crieff, then in Free St. Enoch's, Glasgow ; has edited *Manly Praise* (a book of sacred music for men's voices), etc.

NEWTON, ERNEST (b. 1860), M.A., Cambridge, studied music under Sir George Elvey (Windsor Castle) and Professor Prout, Mus.Doc. (Dublin University). Composer of many well-known songs, the most popular of which are probably *Ailsa Mine*, *Nita Gitana*, and *Going to Kildare* (pp. 22, 24, 28, etc.).

OAKELEY, SIR HERBERT STANLEY (b. 1830), M.A., Oxford, LL.D., Mus.Doc., D.C.L., etc., Emeritus Professor of Music in the University of Edinburgh, composer to Her Majesty in Scotland :

has from the time of his appointment to the Edinburgh Chair, in 1865, taken a warm interest in the subject of students' songs ; has been Hon. President of the Musical Societies of most of the Universities, and has arranged for their use some forty choruses, with orchestral accompaniments ; has published many compositions, vocal and instrumental. " His best work is to be found in his Church Music, which is elaborate yet spontaneous, and which, while it is thoroughly classical in style, has, at the same time, true originality—for instance, his *Service in E Flat*, and his Anthem *Who is this that cometh from Edom ?*—both conceived on a large scale."

OXENFORD, EDWARD (b. 1848), a well-known song writer, librettist, and dramatist ; has, besides translations, produced over 4,500 songs !—is a journalist, and an industrious contributor to many newspapers and magazines.

PATRICK, REV. MILLAR, M.A., St. Andrews, chief editor of this book, was, at his Alma Mater, Secretary of the Students' Union, 1888 ; established, in 1889, *College Echoes*, the University Magazine, and was its first managing editor ; President of the Students' Representative Council, and Chairman of the Students' Union in 1889 ; was, while still a student, in 1891, recommended by the Council for the office of Lord Rector's Assessor in the University Court ; Censor (President of the students) in the United Presbyterian College, Edinburgh, 1893 ; was the originator of the proposal to publish this book, and after laying the plan of it before the St. Andrews Council, and then before the Inter-Universities Conference in Glasgow in 1889, was appointed Convener of the Committee charged with carrying out the scheme. Ordained a minister of the United Presbyterian Church at Biggar, 1894.

QUILLER-COUCH, A. T., a graduate of Oxford, is familiar to all lovers of literature as Q, the author of *The Splendid Spur*, and other romances, and of many delightful volumes of short stories and sketches, in the art of which he is a master, as for example *Noughts and Crosses*, *Wandering Heath*, *The Delectable Duchy*. The song on page 100 is, with his kind permission, taken from his *Green Bays* (Methuen & Co., 1893), and was set to music for this book by Dr. Villiers Stanford.

RALSTON, CLAUDE, a Writer to the Signet, is author of many songs of great popularity in Edinburgh circles. By his kind permission we are able to print one of his latest on page 240.

REID, REV. H. M. B., M.A. (first-class honours, classics), and B.D., St. Andrews ; assistant to Prof. of Humanity there, 1877 ; assistant in Glasgow Cathedral, 1881 ; ordained minister of Balmaghie, Kirkcudbrightshire, 1882. Published, in 1879, a small pamphlet containing a number of Songs (some of them from his own pen) " for the use of St. Andrews students," and was thus one of the pioneers of the movement to provide the students of Scotland with a suitable book of songs. Mr. Reid is a regular contributor to periodical literature, and is author of the following books :—*About Galloway Folk ; The Kirk above Dee Water ; A Cameronian Apostle ; Lost Habits of the Religious Life ; Books that Help the Religious Life ; A Child of the Covenants : a Story of Rullion Green*, etc. (pp. 185, 332, 334).

RORIE, DAVID, M.B., C.M., Edinburgh, late Resident Clinical Assistant, Dundee Royal Asylum. A frequent contributor of verse to the contemporary press (pp. 50 and 346).

SMITH, JOHN, M.D., LL.D., F.R.C.S., etc. Surgeon-Dentist to the Queen in Scotland ; Vice-president of the British Dental Association ; author of various works on the subject of dentistry ; has written many songs, chiefly on subjects connected with medicine and surgery (pp. 26 and 143).

STANFORD, CHARLES VILLIERS (b. 1852), M.A. (honours), Cambridge, Mus.Doc., Oxon. and Cantab, etc. For twenty years conductor of Cambridge University Musical Society ; Professor of Composition and Orchestral Playing, R.C.M., 1883 ; Professor of Music at Cambridge, 1887 ; composer of many Oratorios, Cantatas, and Operas, the best known of his operas being, probably, *Shamus O'Brien* (1896) ; has produced also much Orchestral and Chamber Music of very high quality, and is generally recognised as one of the first of our living composers. Dr. Stanford set the song on page 100 specially for this book.

STEVENSON, ROBERT LOUIS (1850-1894). The best known and best loved of modern men of letters needs no notice here, for who that knows his writings does not also know the man ?—and who, even of those who have not read a word he wrote, does not know his own brave story ? His books, so many and so various, have " engaged and delighted readers of every age, station, and character." Critics and men of letters have vied with each other in the warmth of their admiration of his work, and in their homage to his genius. But, perhaps, the students of Scotland should be— perhaps they are—first among those who cherish pride in him, and affection for his memory. For was he not once, and did he not remain in spirit, one of them ? Mr. Baxter, his friend, in conveying to the editors permission to use the songs on pages 14 and 206, says :—" I know nothing would have gladdened Stevenson's heart more than the idea

that his name should be held in affection by the magnificent raw stuff of which our Scottish students are composed. He loved the life, was of them, with them, and no happier hours were ever passed than in the re-telling of our old student-days' escapades. His name is recorded in the police books, for he passed the bar as defender in one of the snowball riots ! This he and I always considered a niche in the temple of fame."

SYMONDS, JOHN ADDINGTON (1840-95). Educated at Harrow and Balliol, Fellow of Magdalen, Oxford ; a distinguished man of letters, best known by his *Introduction to the Study of Dante*, his great work on *The Renaissance in Italy*, and his *Life of Michael Angelo ;* author of various volumes of poetry, and of translations from Italian poets. Mr. Symonds was in his day the best authority on the subject of mediæval students' songs, many of which he translated, and in the literature and history of which he was deeply and curiously learned. He greeted the project of this book with great enthusiasm, and gave much willing help, by contribution and suggestion, towards carrying it out (pp. 18, 88, and 198).

TERRY, CHARLES SANFORD. Educated at St. Paul's, London, where he was a chorister, and at Clare College, Cambridge, where he graduated with honours in Modern History. After some years spent in school teaching, was appointed Lecturer in History at the Durham College of Science, Newcastle-on-Tyne, where he acts also as Hon. Conductor of the College Musical Society ; has composed music for a considerable number of songs (p. 338).

WALKER, ARCHIBALD STODART, M.B., F.R.C.P., the Edinburgh representative on the Committee of Editors of this book, while at the University held the offices of President of the Union, President of the Students' Representative Council, President of the Dramatic Society, Secretary of the Musical Society, and Editor-in-Chief of *The Student ;* has also been Senior Resident Physician at the Royal Infirmary, Edinburgh ; assistant to the Professor of Physiology and the Professor of Clinical Medicine in the University, and Clinical Assistant at the National Hospital, London, and at the Saltpetrière, Paris ; author of numerous contributions to the medical press on scientific and psychological subjects ; edited, and prefaced by an appreciation, a volume of *The selected Poems of John Stuart Blackie ;* is a frequent contributor also, on literary and philosophical subjects, to the contemporary press (p. 232).

YOUNG, JOHN, C.E. A minor poet of some distinction, author of *Selina, and other Poems*, etc 'p. 52).

Index of Titles.

Index of First Lines.